Married on Purpose

Married on Purpose

A 91 Day Devotional to Ignite
Your Most Intimate
Relationship

BARRY D. HAM PH.D.

Thomas Quinn Nolan Books
A Publication of IFIT

Unless otherwise identified, Scripture quotations are taken from the HOLY

BIBLE, NEW INTERNATIONAL VERSION®. Copyright © 1973, 1978, 1984

Biblica. Used by permission of Zondervan. All rights reserved.

All emphasis within Scripture quotations is the author's own.

Cover design by:Eileen Rockwell

ISBN: **9781795594561**

DEDICATION

This book is dedicated to my wife Andee to whom I am "Married on Purpose." Thanks for your unwavering love and your dedication to doing this journey together..

OTHER BOOKS BY BARRY HAM

Living on Purpose: Knowing God's Design For Your Life

Unstuck: Escaping the Rut of a Lifeless Marriage

God Understands Divorce: A Biblical Message of Grace

CONTENTS

ACKNOWLEDGMENTS

As a book of any substance does not happen in isolation, there are several people to whom I wish to express my deep appreciation. First, are those couples who took the time to read samplings of these devotions and offer their suggestions and feedback. Brad and Kristine, Mike and Teri, Eshcar and Natasha, Ed and Noemi, Paul and Julie, Rich and Keri, and Mike and Monica – I appreciate each of you and count you all as friends.

While you are not the agent on this book, you have been a marvelous agent for my other books and an invaluable source of information and support on this project. Yet, Brad Herman, I am most appreciative of your friendship and you unwavering love for Jesus.

Finally, my partner who devotedly reads and proofs everything I write before it makes its way to the publisher – my wife Andee. Without your love and support and our journey together in serving God, none of this would be possible. Thank you. .

Introduction

If you are reading this, I would assume that you are married or about to be married. And if that is the case, I would ask you – "Why?" Why are you married? Was it like falling into a pothole? In other words it snuck up on you and just sort of happened to you? Or was it an intentional step, something you decided to do on purpose? Whatever your motivation, I hope that you will read this devotional with an eye toward purpose; that you would consider that there are clear reasons for being married.

As a marriage and family therapist, I frequently see the struggles that couples have on a daily basis. Sometimes, these challenges are monumental and threaten the very existence of the marriage. However, the vast majority of stumbling blocks that couples encounter are more of the "have grown complacent" variety.

Most marriages begin with an abundance of hope and promise. But as the years creep by, individuals often grow complacent, taking each other for granted, and eventually cease making any genuine efforts to inject new energy into the marriage. They have, many times, settled into a comfortable existence. Each of them go about their daily routines – fixing meals, going to work, carting the kids off to soccer practice, doing laundry, and collapsing in front of the TV (or now days the cell phone or iPad), crawling into their private existence.

No one meant for the marriage to become, well, so "common" at this point. When people said "I do," each envisioned loved filled meaningful companionship. But here they are – in a marriage that doesn't quite look like what they had originally dreamed it would be.

It is for these relationships that I began writing, in late 2012, a column called "Relationships Tip Tuesdays." This was a marriage resource that was published every Tuesday morning. This book that you are now reading consists of 91 devotionals that have been gleaned and adapted from those years of relationship articles.

It is my hope that you will commit to yourself, and with your spouse, to read one of these each day for the next 91 days. But to be truly effective, it is my desire that you do more than just quickly read one each day – but that you would mull the thoughts over during the day, that you pray about how God might want you to pick up the given topic and possibly make changes in your approach with your husband or wife, and that you would make it a priority to discuss the topics with your mate. A couple of individuals who have reviewed this manuscript prior to publication, have even commented that each day's material is so substantive in concept that a couple might want to work through the book four times in the course of the next year. This could be helpful in both applying and anchoring the principles presented.

Will this commitment be easy? Probably not. Anything that causes us to look intently at areas of our lives that may need transformation is rarely easy. As a matter of fact, we would often rather do anything other than own our own stuff. But here is my promise: if you will commit to putting the effort into this plan for 91 days, your marriage will grow. You will open possibilities of relating to your spouse in new and more energized ways. While I don't know exactly what that will look like, I know that it could possibly take you to that place where you can dream once again - just what this journey might potentially become. And with that perspective, you would grow to be "married on purpose!"

Married On Purpose

Day 1

What Turns Their Crank?

Scripture – "My command is this: Love each other as I have loved you." John 15:12

I love hearing stories about how people are filled; what things lead to feeling valued and cherished – how they get their "crank turned." My wife is a public school administrator. Occasionally, she will get a note from a past student or perhaps a card from a staff member, letting her know what an impact she has had on their education or career. She always comes home and shares those with me. Why? Because, as I listen to the lilt in her voice and see the gleam in her eye, I know that this has "turned her crank."

I wonder today, how do you turn your partner's crank? How do you validate him or let her know that she is cherished? My guess is that it is not by our sarcastic tone or our critical judgments. It is when we love them in a manner that speaks to them – when we love them in their love language. According to author Gary Chapman, that might be in offering words of affirmation, physical touch, gifts, quality time, or deeds of service.

We know what speaks to us – the things that help us to feel loved. But do you know what blesses your significant other? If not, then I encourage you to do two things: 1) endeavor to discover your mate's love language, and 2) creatively speak it. Now, of course, this requires time, thought, and effort. But wouldn't you love to overhear your spouse telling their best friend, "You are not going to believe what he or she did for me today? It blew me away and filled my soul. I am so fortunate to have them." My guess is, hearing that would perhaps even "turn your crank."

Purposeful Action: Make it a point today to love your spouse with your words. Tell a friend or co-worker about a quality you appreciate in your spouse. And even more importantly, be sure to communicate those words of affirmation directly to your mate as well.

Day 2

Are These Preventable Accidents?

Scripture – "Finally, brothers and sisters, whatever is *true, whatever is noble, whatever is right, whatever is pure, whatever is lovely, whatever is admirable—if anything is excellent or praiseworthy—think about such things." Philippians 4:8*

In 2015 the Colorado Department of Transportation reported 15,307 driving crashes in the state that were caused by distracted driving. This was a 16% increase over the previous four years. And, as you might guess, the most significant contributor to the rise in numbers was the cell phone. The spokesman for CDOT stated, "Those who believe in multitasking, that's a myth. You can't be 100 percent focused on driving while you're looking away at passengers or looking at your phones."

Similarly, how many times have you found yourself attempting to talk with your spouse but realize that you are in competition – competing with the newspaper, the TV, the computer, the I-pad, and certainly, the cell phone? How valued do you feel when you are vying for his or her attention but you are not even able to see the whites of their eyes, as they are focused elsewhere? At one time or another, we have all found ourselves in that situation – and we don't like it.

Yet, I can't help but wonder – how frequently our significant others (spouse, kids, relatives) have felt unimportant because our own eyes were distracted and we failed to give them our undivided attention? 15, 307 crashes due to distractions in one year in one state is a frightening number. (As a side note, nationally that number was 1.6 million accidents) If similar statistics were compiled concerning relationships that had crashed and burned due to our distractedness, we might find them equally startling.

I don't know about you, but I don't want my most important relationship to be in danger of crashing because I take my eyes off of it during a critical moment. Let's make a concerted effort today to begin to put to the side those things that are distracting us from the one's whom we love. Instead, endeavor to make them a priority and "think about such things."

Purposeful Action: When your partner speaks with you today, be intentional about making eye contact with them, giving them your full and undivided attention. By your focused attention, create an environment that leads them to feel as if they are the only person in your world.

Day 3

How Do You Fight?

Scripture – "A word aptly spoken is like apples of gold in settings of silver." Proverbs 25:11

People respond in a variety of ways to a question like this. Some might say (because we all want to appear to be reasonable) that they always calmly and rationally discuss disagreements. Others would answer with an honest expression of "We yell at each other, get it all out in the open and then we are fine." And more still might indicate that they avoid arguing at all cost, not sharing feelings, pretending things are fine, and laying low.

There could be lots of different answers. But now here is the question for you that is even more important: Which style of argument or discussion is most often used by loving couples? Think about it for a moment (Jeopardy music is playing in the background) . . . . What was your answer? Ok, so maybe it was a trick question or better yet, maybe it was the wrong question.

Research studies have reported that healthy couples may use any of the styles mentioned above with productive results because the style is not the issue as much as the positive or negative affirmations the individuals experience. The average happy couple has at least five-to-one positive-to-negative interactions during conflict. It doesn't seem to matter whether they are "yellers," "avoiders," or "validators." On the other hand, those couples who are more likely to be headed for divorce are those who experience a 0.8-to-one ratio. Couples who best navigate conflict in constructive ways are those who can balance their arguments with kindness and attentiveness.

I encourage you to focus on making sure that you strive for a five-to-one positive-to-negative ratio when engaged in those difficult discussions in your most important relationships.

Purposeful Action: Unkind words during an argument are easy to do. They require no special skill. However, the next time you encounter a disagreement with your partner, look for the positive in their perspective. Yes, you may still disagree with their position, but acknowledging that their point of view is as valid to them as yours is to you, can go a long ways toward understanding and affirmation. And that leads to healthier marriages.

 *Day 4*

Have You Built a Hedge?

*Scripture – "[Love] always protects, always trusts,
always hopes, always perseveres.
Love never fails. I Corinthians 13:7 & 8a*

When I first moved to Colorado, I planted a row of Ponderosa Pines on the back of my property. My hope was that they would one day grow to create a barrier and with that offer some privacy. You may have planted bushes or built a wooden fence between you and your neighbors in order to accomplish the same thing.

We are pretty good about figuring out how to do that with our homes, but not always as diligent about it with our marriages. If you haven't already, it is time to plant hedges around your heart. Huh? I am talking about protecting your heart.

Think about how fragile and vulnerable our hearts are. They are easily hurt by cruel and thoughtless comments. They are susceptible to feelings of injustice. They can feel anger and they can feel passion. And they are capable of betraying our most important relationships, especially when they have been wounded.

Your commitment to your spouse is unique. It should be unlike any connection you have with any other. And in that, there are things that should be saved for ONLY that person. Yet many of us are careless. Without giving it much thought, we flirt with the opposite sex, we talk disparagingly about our spouse to co-workers, or we share our deepest feelings with someone other than our partner. When we do that, we rob our mate of what should belong solely to him or her. An important principle in protecting our marriages is this idea of building a hedge, a wall of protection around our heart, and in turn, our marriage.

Purposeful Action: Take a look at your marital landscape today. Where is there a break in the hedge that needs to be reinforced? Have you betrayed a confidence with which your spouse entrusted you? If so, apologize. Have you, in frustration, carelessly spoken with a condescending tone of voice? Recommit yourself to speaking to your spouse in a way that protects his or her heart, as well as your own, and in turn, protects your marriage.

Day 5

Did You Ask the Question?

Scripture – "Fools find no pleasure in understanding but delight in airing their own opinions." Proverbs 18:2

My wife has been a public school administrator for many years. Frequently she is confronted with a variety of situations that require additional information. It may have something to do with a Principal needing more information from a parent or a teacher needing clarity around a student issue. Sometimes it is even another administrator who needs additional facts. My wife will frequently ask the person who does not have what they are needing – "Did you ask the question?" Now you may be asking "What question?" The answer is - the question that needs to be asked in order to acquire the needed information. If you are suddenly thinking – "wouldn't that be obvious," you are not the first to do so.

However, this same mistake is made by many of us every day of the week. The number of couples who sit in my office, making behavioral choices with regards to their spouse, based upon faulty assumptions is astounding. One might say, "Well, of course I was angry with him. When I saw that look, I knew he was upset and was going to give me the cold shoulder for not picking up the mail." To which I may respond, "How do you know that?" "I just know," she replies. He proceeds to say, "The look that she saw was my frustration with the credit card company." Yet, they were upset and didn't speak for 24 hours because of assumptions. How could this have been avoided? If someone had ask the question. If she had asked him what the look of frustration was about. If he had asked her what she was angry about. If someone would have "asked the question."

Purposeful Action: It is easy to make assumptions that lead to friction and misunderstandings. But the next time you find yourself about to repeat that mistake – stop. When your spouse says or does something that even has a slight possibility of being interpreted in more than one way – don't assume. Even though you may be convinced, based upon past interactions, that you know what they are thinking, don't do it. Make it your goal to understand their thinking with greater certainty than ever before. And this only will happen if you are willing to **ask the question!**

Day 6

Do You Want to Put Out the Fire?

Scripture – "Do not let any unwholesome talk come out of your mouths, but only what is helpful for building others up according to their needs, that it may benefit those who listen." Ephesians 4:29

I remember when my boys were younger and we would go camping multiple times every summer. We loved to fish, hike, and at night, sit by the campfire and eat s'mores. I recall how much Jeremy, the oldest enjoyed methodically gathering firewood. He would scavenger the area looking for loose limbs, but he most enjoyed finding bigger logs that he could cut up with a saw or chop with his hatchet. The two boys loved building that campfire. At the end of the evening, as we prepared to bed down for the night, we would put out the fire by pouring a couple of buckets of gasoline on it.

WHOA! Stop the presses. We would do what? You mean that isn't what you do to put out a fire? Well of course not – that is ludicrous. And neither did we. We would douse the campfire with water – if we really wanted to put it out. Everyone knows that.

However, when it comes to our relationships, we seem to have forgotten that principle. We get into an argument with our mate. We see that things are getting heated. We know this is not going well and it would be best to de-escalate the situation. So, what do we do – we insult, call names, use sarcasm, and remark how stupid the other person's ideas are. But here is crazy part – we act surprised that they are madder now than when the discussion first began. Really? Yep. Somehow we seem to have forgotten that childhood lesson that throwing gasoline on a fire only increases its size.

When in a heated conversation with our spouse, it is critical that we leave the gasoline (unkind words, etc.) out in the garage. If my goal is for this to go well – it will help if I learn to use "Water words." Things like – "I'm sorry," "I made a mistake," "I guess I miscommunicated," and so on. They can make all the difference in the world.

Purposeful Action: Look for opportunities today to practice firefighting. If you find yourself in a conversation with your partner that begins to get difficult and heats up, slow your thoughts long enough to reach in and grab some of those words and phrases that will dampen the situation. It might even be helpful to let your spouse know what you are doing. Try saying something like, "I can feel this conversation heating up and I love you way too much to start slinging mud and making it worse. So, let me see if I understand my role in this situation right now because I really would like for us to understand each other and be able to do a better job at getting on the same page."

Day 7

How do You Survive the Sharks?

Scripture – "Two are better than one, because they have a good return for their labor: If either of them falls down, one can help the other up." Ecclesiastes 4:9 & 10a

It was supposed to only be a two hour flight from Oahu to the Big Island of Hawaii for two young pilots in their mid-twenties. Dave McMahon and Sydnie Uemoto had never met but were paired to fly this twin engine plane with no passengers. Unexpectedly, they suddenly lost power in both engines, went through their check list in an effort to restart them, and were forced to make a water landing in the ocean.

Miraculously, they survived the crash landing but then were left in the ocean with one working life preserver. Sydnie had a broken nose but managed to follow Dave out of the plane as it quickly filled with water. The short version of the story is that they survived. The struggled through the night with exhaustion, jelly fish stings, and a hovering shark but were finally rescued the next day, after more than 20 hours in the water.

Two sentences jumped out to me about this story. First, was the statement, "To be alone in the ocean was awful and terrifying. But to be with someone else – to feel another person's comforting presence in the darkness – somehow made the ordeal bearable." The second one was after their rescue, "Alone, either of them would have died. But together, they had made it. When one had been weak, the other had been strong."

This story is a picture of marriage. As together we face the battles of raising kids, careers, parent and in-law challenges, and so much more – it was never intended that we face this journey alone. We were meant to have the presence of our partner. We were meant to make "the ordeal bearable."

Purposeful Action: "Sharks" may represent challenges with children, financial struggles, or any number of other potential difficulties. Whether or not you are currently surrounded by them, know that at some point you are likely to be. But rather than wait until you are, reach out to your spouse today and find specific ways that you can be of help to them. Perhaps he or she needs help getting the kids to their sporting events, assistance with paying the bills, or keeping adversarial family at arm's length. Because together you can make it!

 *Day 8*

Do You Remember How to Play?

Scripture – "A cheerful heart is good medicine, but a crushed spirit dries up the bonce." Proverbs 17:22

A couple recently sat in my office – intense, unhappy, and bearing down on their marriage with the same exertion required to open a very tight jar. In other words, they were working really really hard but were not having success. The marriage was no longer fulfilling and they both felt unable to meet the desires and expectations of their mate. This was not fun.

It wasn't just that it was no longer fun. They truly seemed to have forgotten how to have fun. This is not uncommon. It is much like the person who takes up golf because they enjoy the sport. But before long they are becoming more and more self-critical with every swing until they finally heave the golf club into the woods in frustration. Similarly, couples can begin to approach their spousal interactions with the same "bearing down" attitude used in approaching the 9th hole.

Back to the couple in my office. This intense place was where they were – and it was exhausting for them. I asked them to shelve their issues for one week. During that week they were to simply enjoy each other. We weren't pretending that the issues weren't there. We were just, as Bob says in the movie, "What About Bob," "taking a vacation from their problems." I offered some suggestions of ways that could do this and be more playful.

It was refreshing to see them a week later with smiles on their faces. One afternoon, while sitting on the deck, things got a little too serious. So the wife pulled out squirt guns she had purchased at the store that week. She told her husband, "If you don't want your laptop to get wet, you had better put it inside." Totally caught off guard, he did. Then before handing him his pistol, she squirted him first and then things were off and running.

Purposeful Action: Playfulness can be the catalyst for renewed intimacy. If possible, locate a picture from some past event or outing when you and your mate were having fun and reminisce. Talk about what you most enjoyed about those times and possible aspects that might be fun to recreate. Then if you are feeling bold and brave (and it doesn't have to be a squirt gun), surprise your mate with some zany behavior that he or she fell in love with. It could be fun.

 *Day 9*

Radical Acceptance

*Scripture – "Accept one another, then, just as Christ
accepted you, in order to bring praise to God."*
Romans 15:7

I recently heard a client make the statement, "My
husband doesn't accept me." When I asked for her to
give me more information, she went into a lengthy
list: "I go to bed too early, I don't vacuum correctly, I
take too long getting ready in the morning, I don't set the
table the right way" . . . and on and on the list went.

She even indicated that her desires weren't correct. When
I asked her to explain, she said that her husband had
purchased all of the furniture in the house. As I turned to
him with an inquiring look, he replied with surprise,
stating, "We went together and bought the furniture." She
responded with, "Yes, we went together, but when I told
you what I liked, you told me how that isn't really what I
like and that you know best what I want." It was easy to
see that this wife did not feel valued and accepted.

I sometimes see a husband or wife who has taken it upon
themselves to rectify a perceived deficiency in their
spouse. I have yet to find a man or woman who
appreciates that approach. When our spouse appears to
come at us from a more "correct" perspective, we begin
to feel not good enough and perhaps even resentful. But

what if you came to your spouse with an attitude of radical acceptance?

Purposeful Action: Perhaps you already fully accept your spouse's quirks, idiosyncrasies, and unique ways of doing things – or at least you think you do. But I want to suggest that to really know if that is true – ask them. Ask your husband or wife for an example of when they feel the most relaxed and most emotionally safe with you. This will give you a clue. At the same time, ask them for an example of when they feel most judged by you. Don't get defensive, because we all need work in this area. Simply listen, learn, and chart a course of new behaviors where needed.

 *Day 10*

What Kind of Love Do You Have?

Scripture – "Be devoted to one another in love. Honor one another above yourselves." Romans 12:10

"When we stood there getting married, I remember the preacher saying, 'For better, for worse; in sickness, and in health." I was 20 years old and I thought, I wonder what 'in sickness and in health means. I thought, he'll have a stroke in 40 years; I can do that." – Darnly Motter

Many of us may have stood with our husband or wife to be and thought something similar. As long as, "sickness, poorer, or worse" was waaay down the road, further than we could imagine – it seemed doable. For Darnly Motter, sickness came 9 years later when they had two children and she was pregnant with their third.

Driving home from dinner, Darnly and her husband Larry were hit head-on by a 16 year old drunken driver who had also used drugs. The kids were fine and Darnly had a few broken bones. But Larry lost his memories and with that, much of his life. Initially hoping to see progress, his wife eventually learned that she had to accept Larry as he was.

While he can still be loving and funny – he will never remember to do the small things such as getting his wife flowers or chocolates on Valentine's Day. And yet, his wife doesn't allow that to derail her. She clearly states that they celebrate a different kind of love: commitment. "It's a love that's a decision. It's a decision to do the best thing you can for somebody else." "My whole goal, my whole life was to make Larry the best he can be with what he has."

For some, it is learning to deal with a sick spouse; perhaps for others – a child with a disability. Or it may be that we are simply still learning to deal with petty differences or irritating behaviors. But whatever our situation – we are summoned to this decision called "love."

Purposeful Action: Today may be one of those days when your spouse is "lovable" or it may be one that it is all you can do to be in the same room with each other. But it doesn't really matter because somewhere along the way, you made a "commitment" to love them. It may sound noble on the global front but can be much more challenging at the daily level. Decide today to accept your spouse as the "best he or she can be with what they have." Regardless of whether you are faced with a significant or minor issue, demonstrate this acceptance in a concrete way.

Day 11

Are You a Victim of Technoference?

Scripture – "Martha, Martha," the Lord answered, 'You are worried and upset about many things, but few things are needed—or indeed only one. Mary has chosen what is better, and it will not be taken away from her." Luke 10:41-42

C hicago psychologist, Nicole Martinez reported that in a study of young married women, "70 percent reported that face-to-face conversations were stopped in their tracks by a partner's phone use or even active texting." These intrusions have been referred to by some as "technoference."

Technology impacts relationships in a variety of ways. Recognizing our increasing dependence on our internet world, it is easy to see how we, or our significant others, can be together and yet feel excluded, isolated, and alone.

Study after study, such as the 2014 Pew Research survey, report that increasing numbers of couples are experiencing conflict related to mobile devices. A research team from Virginia Tech observed couple's conversations in a coffee shop setting and reported what they called "the iPhone Effect." Merely having a smartphone present, even if not is use – just on the table

– degraded private conversations, causing partners to be "less willing to disclose deep feelings and less understanding of each other."

While these experiences aren't new, they are increasingly invading our relational world. When a wife found it difficult to pry her husband's attention away from a football game on television, at least when they left the TV, that distraction was set aside. But in today's culture, we no longer leave the technology behind – we take it with us <u>everywhere.</u> And therefore, its incessant intrusion is seldom further than our finger tips.

Purposeful Action: Be intentional about engaging in personal face-to-face interactions with your spouse, while leaving the phone on silent in a completely different room. Your husband or wife deserves having you be fully present. So, put the smart phone away and give them 100% of your attention.

Day 12

How You Say It

Scripture – "The mouth of the righteous person
utters wisdom, and his tongue speaks what is just."
Psalm 37:30

Have you ever been told that the problem with your communication is not what you say but how you say it? Most of us have heard that at one time or another. Because we may not choose the best phrase or words, what we say is misunderstood and our best intentions go by the wayside. Author Scott Sells discusses questions that we can ask our teens that demonstrate our openness, humility, and true desire to cooperate. As I read these, I thought about how appropriate these questions (with a little modification) can be for couples whose communication patterns have become closed and hostile. Let me share four questions with you.

1. **How come you have not thrown in the towel yet and given up on me and our relationship? What keeps you going?** This shows humility, ownership of your issues, and openness to your spouse.

2. **I have told you in the past how you can be helpful to me. Now I want know how can I be helpful to you?** For some of you, you may have to wait until your spouse picks his or her jaw up

off of the floor, before they can respond. They may not have heard this kind of question in a long time – but they will welcome it.

3. **What things have I done or said in the past that were not helpful or turned you off? I ask this question because I don't want to repeat the same mistakes in the future.** If your communication in the past has closed down your partner's spirit – this will certainly contribute (if it is sincere) to opening them up again.

4. **If we were on track to solving some long-standing problems that we have (you might want to be specific about an issue), what do you see me doing differently to help this happen?** Once again, showing non-defensive openness can go a long ways in reopening closed hearts.

Purposeful Action: Which questions do you most need to be asking your husband or wife today to reopen healthy communication? Select one question, find a time when you both have a few minutes without interruption, and dive in. Being vulnerable in this manner can be a little intimidating, but the care it is likely to communicate to your spouse is priceless.

 *Day 13*

Situational Blindness

Scripture – "Do not conform to the pattern of this world, but be transformed by the renewing of your mind. Then you will be able to test and approve what God's will is—his good, pleasing and perfect will."
Romans 12:2

I recently read a story about a couple in Oregon who were traveling back home from an out of town trip. They were using their GPS as they navigated an unfamiliar route. Nearing a small town, their GPS instructed them to turn off onto a little used forest road. This was a result of their GPS being programmed to take the "shortest route" as opposed to the "quickest route." As they continued down roads that were covered deeper and deeper with snow, they became stuck – got unstuck – and then continued on down the same path. Eventually, they were completely stuck, could not get a cell phone signal, and huddled in their car for three days until a sheriff's deputy rescued them.

You may have heard stories of this nature that are the result of individuals blindly trusting their technological device in spite of the signs that should have led to different choices. Sometimes the consequences are tragic.

Relationships can sometimes follow a similar course. Communication breaks down, conflict arises, harsh words are exchanged, loving actions are sidelined – and we find ourselves heading down a dangerous forest road. While our situation demands that we change course – we often continue doing what we have always done. We continue to take our friend's weak advice that has rarely proved beneficial. We listen to our culture's pop influence even as the wheels continue to come off the relationship.

It is during these times that it is helpful to be aware of just how easy it is to be situationally blind and headed for a cliff. This is when it is good to stop – survey our relational surroundings and do something different.

Purposeful Action: Ask yourself, "in what ways am I rigidly following a course of action that is actually hurting instead of benefiting my marriage?" Be willing to consider that you may be heading in the wrong direction and change course. If you are uncertain whether this is the case or not, ask your spouse if he or she sees any areas where you appear to be more committed to a course of action than you are to them. Then carefully and non-defensively – listen.

Day 14

What are Your Unspoken Rules?

Scripture – "We who are strong ought to bear with the failings of the weak and not to please ourselves. Each of us should please our neighbors for their good, to build them up." Romans 15:1-2

When reading that question you may think, "I don't have any unspoken rules," and perhaps you don't – now. But my suspicion is that you probably have a few, and when you were first married you had a ton of them. You see "unspoken rules" are those ways that we have of doing things that we naively assume everybody has.

For example, when dinner is over – who does this dishes? If you were raised in a household where "mom always did the dishes," or "whoever didn't cook did the dishes," or "we just let them pile up in the sink until it was full before we did the dishes," then you have experienced what became "unspoken rules." We all have them. And this is not necessarily a problem – until you are in a significant relationship.

We all bring to the table our assumptions about how life ought to work. And while we might not tell our partner that our way of doing things is best, we probably secretly think that it is. Unfortunately, this attitude is usually made evident by our sighs, eye-rolls, or our snarky responses. Then the trouble starts.

While my wife was raised doing things a certain way and I grew up (some might take issue with that) performing tasks in a different manner – what matters now is – how do my wife and I want to conduct things in our household with our family. It is important that we set aside "what has been" as we together determine "what will be."

Purposeful Action: Identify one issue that repeatedly comes up as an irritating difference between you and your partner. Is it possible that this difference could be attributed to an unexpressed unspoken rule? If so, confess this to your mate. Then ask clarifying questions in order to better understand their perspective on this same issue.

Day 15

Conflict

Scripture – "My dear brothers and sisters, take note of this: Everyone should be quick to listen, slow to speak and slow to become angry." James 1:19

I know couples who seem to fight all the time. Some are always on the verge of walking out, while others would label their marriage as very happy. What is the difference? It may be in how we approach conflict. Unless we are exactly like the person we are in a relationship with (in which case, one of us is unnecessary), we are going to have conflict. Many are afraid of conflict and think it is a bad thing. Others see it as an opportunity to learn from each other, come to better understandings, and grow both individually and in the relationship.

You may think, "You make it sound like it should somehow be easy – yet it is anything but that." I completely get that. We have all experienced what I would call "over-the-top, nightmare conflict." However, even in the midst of difficult conflict, and I truly know what that looks like, I want to suggest 5 tips that might be helpful in moving conflict in a positive direction.

First, try to address the issue as quickly as possible. Some things cannot be addressed immediately. But to prevent differences from festering, resolution sooner rather than later is helpful.

Second, refrain from name calling. All that this really does is give us an element of hurtful control and widens the gap that you are already feeling. Name calling never serves to move us closer to solving the issue.

Third, don't intimidate. Individuals will default to this tactic when they feel they are losing an argument and they want to win at all costs. Remember – resolution is your goal.

Fourth, don't deflect – stick to the subject. It is so easy to get off on tangents – especially when the current topic is not working to your advantage. Work diligently to stay focused on the current issue.

Finally, remember that your partner is not the enemy. Whether you have been married 35 years or are newlyweds – whether you have kids at home or they are grown and out on their own – remember that you are in this together. It is important that you focus on the fact that you are a "we." Instead of battling against each other, focus on battling for "us."

Purposeful Action: We married someone who is different from ourselves because we valued qualities and perspectives that we were lacking. Identify one such quality in your spouse and, during the course of your day, text or email them your appreciation for the richness this adds to your life.

Day 16

How Do You Support?

Scripture – "Do not withhold good from those to whom it is due, when it is in your power to act."
Proverbs 3:27

There is a story told that "Following a parade, the mayor of a large American city was walking with his wife when they passed a man sweeping the streets. The wife recognized the street sweeper as one of her old high school boyfriends. The three had a short conversation before the mayor and his wife continued on their way. Halfway down the street the mayor leaned over to his wife and whispered, 'Just think, if you had married him, today you'd be the wife of a street sweeper.' His wife smiled and whispered back, 'No, if I had married him, today he'd be the mayor.'"

While this humorous story is most likely fictitious, it does a great job of illustrating a powerful point. People will rise to our level of expectations. When they (our spouse, our children – and just about any relationship), are treated with love and respect, and are offered support – they will rise to our expectations, frequently exceeding their initial abilities. But the opposite is also true. If we are condescending and demeaning, offering no support – individuals will sink to the level of our expectations as well – dropping below what most believed that person was capable of. The statement has been made that "behind every great man is a great woman." I would modify that to say that behind every achieving individual is a supportive fan club. This truism has been demonstrated in the lives of spouses and children time and time again.

So my question is simple – how are you supporting those whom you most care about? Are you loving them in a manner that encourages them and lifts them to new heights?

Purposeful Action: Consider today something you may not have been able to achieve were it not for the support of your spouse. Tell them of your gratefulness and ask, "What is one specific area where I could be of better support to you as you strive to attain your goals?" Based on what they expressed, endeavor to support them in tangible ways.

Day 17

What Kind of Agent are You?

Scripture – "Each of you should use whatever gift you have received to serve others, as faithful stewards of God's grace in its various forms." I Peter 4:10

For some, flying is a relatively pleasant experience. For others it is stressful and may even require anti-anxiety medicine. Regardless of which category you find yourself in, the trip can either be positively or negatively impacted before you ever leave the ground, when you encounter the ticket agent.

You may have encountered, as I have, an agent who seemed as though they had just spent the last 8 hours trying to sleep in economy class. They didn't smile, they weren't very helpful, and they only did the minimum to deal with your concerns – in hopes that you would quickly go away so that they could disregard the next person in line.

Over a Thanksgiving holiday break, my wife and I were returning on a flight from out of state. As I pulled the rental car up to drop my wife off with the luggage, an agent (it was an outdoor ticket counter) quickly came over and asked me if I was returning a rental car. I replied that I was and I would be right back to take care of the bags. She said, "No hurry. I will take care of your bags and if you will just let me take a peek at your driver's license, I will go ahead and get the boarding passes for you and your wife." Wow! Now that is what I call going out of your way to serve someone.

If I were to ask your spouse which kind of agent you are, what would he or she say? Ponder that for a moment . . . .

Purposeful Action: Determine to serve your spouse today with the "go after it" attitude with which my agent served me. Perhaps that could be reflected by getting up 5 minutes early to bring your husband or wife coffee in bed; unloading the dishwasher quickly rather than waiting for your mate to do it; or taking the initiative to plan a dinner date without being asked to do so. You see, your spouse is . . . well, your spouse. Shouldn't we serve our mate with at least the same attitude that this agent offered me?

Day 18

Shopping and Snowshoeing

Scripture – "And over all these virtues put on love,
which binds them all together in perfect unity."
Colossians 3:14

What do you enjoy doing? It might be hiking, watching football, sipping tea, or flower gardening. We all have interests of some kind, with some being quite unique. One of my sons used to be a veterinary technician. When he first began school to pursue that career field, I think that he figured he would enjoy working with cats, dogs, and other animals. However, as he got into it, he discovered an unknown love for fish – freshwater, saltwater, all kinds of fish. As a result his aquarium collection continued to proliferate.

Husbands and wives also have varied interests – and sometimes the differences of those preferred hobbies can lead to extremely separate lives. In order to combat that drift, I have seen couples make very intentional efforts in joining together to pursue common activities. Certainly they maintain separate hobbies as well, but by learning the art of self-sacrifice, they have discovered an entirely new level of connection and intimacy.

My wife is not a big snow activity person – such as skiing or making snow angels in the snow. Therefore, snowshoeing did not initially sound appealing to her. Yet, when she went with me, she discovered that she loved it and now we share this activity frequently in the winter months. As a guy, shopping at Home Depot intrigues me – clothes shops and boutiques, not so much. However, when we go on trips, I have learned to shoe shop, clothes shop, and home furnishing shop with my wife. While I may sometimes look for the "husband's chair" as I call it, while she explores, I have grown to enjoy those outings with her.

You see, it is not really about the activity as much as it is about being together. We continue to find fresh ways to enjoy doing meaningful things together and, more importantly, to simply enjoy each other's presence.

Purposeful Action: Sit down with your partner and make a list of things that you each enjoy. Find three things that you could try and engage in together. However, make the focus to relish your time with each other. Now, turn that list into reality by actually implementing your three items.

 *Day 19*

Have You Started Dating?

Scripture – "Though one may be overpowered, two can defend themselves. A cord of three strands is not quickly broken." Ecclesiastes 4:12

If you are single and are dating, the answer to the above question is a resounding "Yes!" However, others may be inclined to say, "Nope. I quit dating 25 years ago when I got married." While I understand the thinking, I would contend that rather than marriage be the end of dating it should instead be that which solidifies dating.

Unfortunately, dating often gets pushed to the side. I think about my oldest son and his wife. He works full-time, she part-time, as they endeavor to have one of them at home with their nearly 3 year old daughter and their 1 year old son. With young children come a host of new expenses. Life is full and some days feel like a struggle just to keep their heads above water with regard to energy level, finances, and getting diapers changed and people fed. The idea of a date night is probably the last thing on their mind. They are probably happy to just collapse on the couch for five minutes.

Couples who carve out time for one another have healthier relationships. Not rocket science, I know. Before we were married, dating was a priority. We worked diligently to find time for each other. We coveted those precious times of talking and connecting and doing fun things together. But then we got married. We got busy. We had kids. We got tired.

The principle of continuing to date my spouse, especially after we are married, is an important one. It doesn't have to be expensive or elaborate but it does have to be intentional. This is not a time to talk about the kids, finances, school supplies, etc., but is a time to focus on and enjoy each other. Studies have reported that those couples who spend time alone each week experience three time higher levels of happiness, positive communication, and sexual satisfaction than those who don't make this time a priority.

So, regardless of what has been the norm up to now, if you want to get out of the rut of your relationship, if you want to breathe new life into your marriage, if you want to take steps to create a cord whose strands are not "quickly broken" – make it a priority to begin dating your spouse.

Purposeful Action: This will be fairly straight forward – ask your spouse out on a date (unless they are asleep) right now. It can be as simple as a coffee date. Turn to them, call them, or text them. But ask them to join you in some intentional time together.

 *Day 20*

How Do You Like Your Touch?

Scripture – "Do everything in love."
I Corinthians 16:14

In this installment, I want to talk about sex – well, sort of. I want to encourage you with a brief look at how to better crawl into connection with your spouse. While that may seem strangely phrased to you, I am wanting you to picture getting into a place of safety. Perhaps as a child you had a favorite tree house, closet, or bed where you could just crawl up into it, snuggle up with a stuffed animal or blanket, and just safely relax. When you were able to do this, your body lost all of its tension and you were able to truly embrace and enjoy the moment.

James Coan, a University of Virginia neuroscientist, contends that being able to find this kind of safety in connection is an essential ingredient to healthy intimacy. In his brain imaging work, he has been able to see the things that cause stress, consume attention, and drain people of energy. When we experience the stress of work and other distractions, we become self-involved and have difficulty being in the moment with our spouse.

But here is the powerful lesson – when we do something

as simple as hold our husband or wife's hand, a soothing effect takes place. As Coan states, "It's like magic. Calm washes over the whole brain." And when that happens, we are able to move into a place of less self-focus and greater readiness to play. The touch of our partner allows us to offload things that are irrelevant.

I hear people, usually women, complain "that the only time my husband touches me is when he wants sex." This creates tension and resentment. But when couples touch with no agenda, an entirely different effect takes place.

Purposeful Action: Do you want better intimacy with your spouse? Right now, or at least before the day is over, initiate non-sexual touch with your mate. This could be a hug, holding their hand, or simply putting your arm around them as you watch TV. It may not alter the dynamics all it once, but I am confident that it is the first step towards an improved connection.

 *Day 21*

The Best is Yet to Come!

Scripture – "Therefore, if anyone is in Christ, the new creation has come: The old has gone, the new is here!" 2 Corinthians 5:17

It is your child's birthday. You have purchased a new bike that he has been talking and dreaming about non-stop. But first you bring out his favorite cake with candles lit and ready for him to blow out. He proclaims, "I love this kind of cake. Thank you. This is great!" You respond with, "You're welcome but the best is yet to come!"

We have experienced this with gifts, vacations, and maybe even aspects of our jobs – but how about in our marriages? Far too often, I sit with couples who have been married 10, 15, even 20 years as they talk about their marriage as though it is a past event. Discussing how they met, or the excitement and intensity of their love in those early years seems but a distant memory. Truly they get stuck in thinking that goes – "It was wonderful then, it is awful now, and it can never get any better."

But what if the best is yet to come? Regardless of the difficulties you have experienced – critical words, betrayal, even unfaithfulness – where you are right now is not where you have to remain. I have witnessed couples recover from the most horrific of experiences to find themselves in the best place they have been in 20 years. But in order to do this, they first had to pry themselves out of their "this is good as it gets" mentality. Couples who have found happiness and fulfillment with their spouse have been able to adopt a mindset of, "the best is yet to come." While I am not suggesting that some kind of "Pollyannaish" perspective will make the world right, I do believe that a "best is yet to come" focus opens the door to possibilities.

Purposeful Action: Have a conversation with your partner, focusing on two thoughts: 1) what has been the highlight of our life together during the course of our marriage? (it can't be the kids or grandkids – it has to be about the two of you), and 2) If we were to dream, what would you like to plan and look forward to in the future? You see, if you turn your gaze from the rear view mirror in your relationship to a forward focus out the windshield, you could discover that the "best" just might lie ahead.

 *Day 22*

Are You Looking in the Right Light?

Scripture – "For where your treasure is, there your heart will be also." Matthew 6:21

I recently read a story written by Dr. Bo Brock, a Texas veterinarian, about his grandparents. It seems that his grandmother would sprinkle his granddad's work pants with starch and iron them every day. This struck Bo as odd, because, as a farmer, many days his Papaw would not see another person the entire day. Ironing his work pants just didn't make any sense.

One day when Bo was about 13 he asked his grandmother about this practice. In his mind, those pants were going to quickly get dirty and he just couldn't understand why she would invest the time. She replied that "Papaw was the most handsome man in the world. She said he was her best friend and the love of her life. She loved every chance she got to show him off and make the rest of the world jealous that he was hers. She went on to say, 'You just never know when Papaw might run into someone and I want him to look the part of the most handsome man God ever made."

As Bo looked at his granddad, he saw a skinny man with thinning hair and crooked false teeth, He could not understand what his grandmother was thinking and he told her so.. She responded with, "You just aren't looking in the right light."

How we view our mate says a lot about what is important to us and our relationships. How do you see your spouse? Do you see them as fat, skinny, old, wrinkled, with a body out of shape – or do you see the most handsome man or the most beautiful woman in the world? I would submit that many of us may need to make sure we are "looking in the right light."

Purposeful Action: When you married, you probably thought that you had landed the most beautiful or handsome person on the planet. While the years change our physical appearance, that person you married is still inside there. How you view them is your choice – it is up to you. If you choose to see them as the "most handsome man God ever made," you will truly begin to relate to them that way. Choose to treasure him or her, and your heart will soon follow. Begin to do this today by telling them as well as proclaiming to others, the fabulous catch you have made.

Day 23

Free!

Scripture – "And the two will become one flesh. So they are no longer two, but one flesh." Mark 10:8

"What an eye opening experience," is the thought that went through my mind. I have read about it, I've seen it, and I have written about it. But I recently experienced it at a new level. "What is that?" you are wondering. Having my cell phone off.

You see, my wife and I were recently out of the country and my cell phone didn't have any service. Oh, I could have purchased some kind of an international plan for a week, but it didn't seem necessary. And besides, I thought it would be nice to be detached from it for a few days. This first 24 hours were the most interesting. Every time I felt the slightest vibration, I reached for my pocket with the phone in it. I continually reached for my phone thinking I had better check e-mail or perhaps Facebook. But it was turned off.

Finally, I took the phone out of my pocket and locked it in the hotel safe – I mean, after all, I had no service so I shouldn't be needing it. For the next 24 hours my pocket felt empty and I would have brief moments of panic, thinking I had lost or misplaced my phone. I couldn't believe what a slave I had become to that electronic device.

By the time 72 hours had gone by, I no longer was driven to find and check the phone. I was FREE. Free to enjoy my vacation, free to focus on my wife, free to relax – completely relax. And oh how wonderful it was. It was a terrific experience that I can't wait to replicate. Of course, now that I am back home and in the daily routines, the phone is reattached in its regular place – reattached in my pocket, and more significantly, reattached in my psyche.

But I realized that it is not necessary for me to leave the country to have this experience. I can have it here.

Purposeful Action: Set aside times to leave the phone in the other room, times with your spouse, your family, your friends, when you say – "You are more important right now in this moment and I am declaring that by not having my phone on or anywhere nearby." It sounds good in theory, but detaching can be intimidating. Designate a time or location today that will be a phone free zone.

Day 24

Intention vs. Consequence

Scripture – "The one who has knowledge uses words with restraint, and whoever has understanding is even-tempered." Proverbs 17:27

I recently sat with a couple in my office as they described a conflict they encountered. It seems that the husband and wife had agreed to meet at a restaurant for dinner one evening. The husband was held up at a meeting that ran long and arrived about a half hour late. This was not the first time that this kind of thing had happened, as a matter of fact, it was a regular occurrence. So, it was easy to understand when the wife expressed her displeasure. The husband apologized and said "I didn't mean to be late." His wife coldly responded with "You never mean to be late."

As the icicles hung in the air, the husband thought that since he had apologized, things should be fine. But they weren't – and here is why. They were each looking at the situation through a different set of lenses. He was seeing it through the lens of "intention." He wasn't making her wait on purpose. He intended to get there on time. Therefore, since he had good intentions – she should forgive him and all would be peachy. And they might have been if she were using that lens. However, she is viewing things through a different one – that of consequence. Regardless of the reason for being late, the reality is – she had to wait for a half hour. He experienced the situation from his own perspective – good intentions. On the other hand, she experienced it through feeling discounted and unimportant. It would seem that it is NOT the thought that counts, but the action.

Purposeful Action: The next time your spouse is upset with you – begin the discussion by acknowledging how your behaviors impacted him or her. The other person really doesn't care much at that point what your intentions were. They want to know that you understand how your actions affected them. Listen to their perspective and endeavor to view things through their lens of understanding.

 *Day 25*

Mitigation

Scripture – "You were taught, with regard to your former way of life, to put off your old self, which is being corrupted by its deceitful desires; to be made new in the attitude of your minds; and to put on the new self, created to be like God in true righteousness and holiness.
Therefore each of you must put off falsehood and speak truthfully to your neighbor, for we are all members of one body." Ephesians 4:22-25

Mitigation is probably not a word that we hear or use a great deal. But in Colorado, particularly in 2012 and 2013, it is a word that was used quite a bit. In June of 2013 began the Black Forest Fire, the worst wildfire in Colorado history, resulting in the loss of over 500 homes and two lives. In reading numerous articles regarding the fire, I was intrigued by forecasts the experts had been making about fires in Colorado. They indicated that the increase in dangerous fires was not surprising as trees had grown, needles and vegetation had accumulated, and many had not taken steps to clear out some of these potential fuels – they had not been doing fire mitigation. Others had been intentional about doing mitigation work and their homes were better protected in case of fire. Now please don't misunderstand me, when a fire like the Black Forest fire hits, for some homes – no amount of mitigation would have prevented their destruction. Yet, for others, fire mitigation may have saved their homes.

The lesson that I observed from this is that many in relationships need to do better mitigation. By this I mean, removing irritants and obstacles from the relationships; getting rid of language that fuels conflict; building hedges of protection around the marriage that solidify faithfulness; being honest and forthright to keep lines of communication clear. I have seen many marriages end where no one was surprised. The seeds of destruction had been sown for years with nothing done to combat them. Yet, I can't help but wonder – had the individuals in the relationship done better clearing of destructive fuels – better mitigation along the way, what might the result have been? When a wildfire breaks out – it is too late to do mitigation. What can you begin to do today to clear the fuels that have the power to harm your relationship?

Purposeful Action: Begin your own mitigation with something basic such as the words that you use in communicating with your loved one. It is easy to become careless in the things we say and the tone of voice that we use. Strive to run things through a filter of "If my spouse were speaking to me with the words and tone that I am using with him or her, would I feel valued?" If so, you are on the right track. But if in doubt, rethink your words so that you are removing obstacles rather than placing new ones into the relationship.

Day 26

Is it on Purpose?

Scripture – "A person may think their own ways are right, but the Lord weighs the heart." Proverbs 21:2

I t Is 3:00 AM and it is starting again . . . his snoring. You lay in bed getting more irritated by the minute. Part of your irritation is because you can't sleep, which of course contributes to you being tired, which in turn contributes to your irritation. The longer you listen to the snoring, slowly you become convinced that he is doing this because he is uncaring, selfish, and doesn't want you to get any sleep. As a matter of fact, you are pretty sure he is doing this on purpose.

Now putting this in print in the light of day may expose the absurdity of the argument. But in the darkness at 3:00 AM, the thoughts somehow seem coherent. However, if you are to keep yourself from whacking him with a pillow (or whatever else may be handy), it is essential that you address his intent; and here it is . . . he is sleeping. In all likelihood, there is no intent associated with the snoring.

Psychologist Michael Cunningham from the University of Louisville likens irritating behaviors to allergies. When we are first exposed to an allergen in the air, we typically have a mild reaction. But by the hundredth exposure, we may be coughing and wheezing. Similarly, the first time your partner leaves a cabinet door open, it is no big deal –

it may even seem cute, but after repeated incidents (especially if you have brought it to his or her attention), you lose your cool.

This is why those in lengthy relationships can seem to explode over the tiniest of infractions.

While I realize that some individuals use irritants as a way to have power in a relationship, I find that more often than not, annoying behaviors are more likely to reflect a difference in how we approach the world.

Purposeful Action: The next time your spouse demonstrates one of those irritating behaviors (or when he or she notices ones that you produce), try using them as an opportunity to discuss intent. Many times what seems intentional might be a mere lack of awareness or thoughtlessness. Invite the other person to describe their perceptions, as you listen for understanding. At the same time, work to be more sensitive and thoughtful by owning your own behaviors that may stir irritation. Be quick to apologize but slow to accuse.

Day 27

How Do You Clear Out Emotional Gunk?

Scripture – "Bear with each other and forgive one another if any of you has a grievance against someone. Forgive as the Lord forgave you."
Colossians 3:13

Marriages struggle. Ok – not a profound statement in a world where marriages are falling apart all around us. But it is still a true statement. Whether I am at a Men's Bible Study or running into friends at the store, a common question that I get asked is, "How can I make my marriage better? Is there a secret?"

My first response is – "No, there is no secret." But I follow that up with, "But there are certainly steps you can take to lay a solid foundation that will help to develop a vibrant marriage." I want to take today to look at one of the bricks for this foundation.

Most relationships start out positively enough, but before long that become gunked up with unresolved crud (I know – not real clinical terms). And if left unresolved, walls of resentment begin to build. To begin to build a solid foundation for your relationship, it is essential that you begin to clear away the relational clutter. This starts with forgiveness – with wrapping grace all around this relationship.

When we find ourselves stuck in resentment and stubbornness, it is difficult to express any tenderness or compassion. Instead we snip at our spouse over issues that aren't the real issues, we talk to them condescendingly, we undermine their attempts to grow, and the list goes on. But forgiveness clears the path for the possibility of a restored relationship. When we are willing to forgive, we create a softness with our spouse that better prepares us to resolve conflicts, as well as paves the road for greater emotional and physical intimacy.

Purposeful Action: Taking an internal inventory, take hold of one unresolved issue that is causing you to harbor resentment toward your partner. If it can be addressed and resolved, by all means do it. But if it is an issue that seems engraved in stone, consider laying the issue before God, letting go of the pent up hostilities, and heaping love on your spouse in some tangible way. He or she is worth much more than the emotional gunk.

Day 28

Touch

Scripture – "Truly I tell you, anyone who will not receive the kingdom of God like a little child will never enter it." [16] And he took the children in his arms, placed his hands on them and blessed them."
Mark 10:15-16

Touch is an amazing communication tool that is frequently overlooked in marriage. Now that may seem a strange comment. I mean, we think of marriage and we think of hand-holding, kissing, and sexual intimacy – we think of touch. But touch is not just limited to romantic touch.

I recently had lunch with a pastor from Vietnam. We were discussing marriage characteristics in this country as well as those in Vietnam. Touch, or lack thereof, was one item that caught my attention. It has not been uncommon for a couple in that country to have been married for decades and have never kissed or held hands. While there have been some cultural reasons that have contributed to that, the relational impact has been huge. As they have helped people to learn to touch one another, the changes beginning to take place in the marriages have been overwhelming.

When people touch (we're not talking about sex here, but hugs, touching the arm or shoulder, and so on), their oxytocin levels go up and their heart rates go down. We even reap some of the same benefits when we are the initiator of touch. Touching is one of the most fundamental ways of fostering communication with your partner. And how reciprocal the touch is can tell you a lot about the relationship. Depending on the stage of marriage where a couple finds themselves, their reciprocal touch may be more or it may be less. But over time, couples usually adjust to each other's touching habits and comfort zone. If they are unable to do this, it has been known to derail the relationship. Couples who are more satisfied with their relationship tend to touch more. However, a true indicator of long-term health is really around how often your partner touches you in response to your initial touch. As one researcher stated, "The stronger the reciprocity, the more likely someone is to report emotional intimacy and satisfaction with the relationship."

Purposeful Action: Regardless of where touch is in your relationship – take it from where it is. If you almost never touch, then make it a point to give a reassuring squeeze on the arm or an arm around the shoulder hug. If you are already doing those things, then perhaps reach out while watching TV to hold your mate's hand. Whatever your level of touch, take it one notch up and see how this can improve your connection.

Day 29

Pull Together

Scripture – "From him the whole body, joined and held together by every supporting ligament, grows and builds itself up in love, as each part does its work." Ephesians 4:16

In the beginning of our marriage, we probably said, as a part of our wedding vows, "For better for worse." Very simply, we declare these words to our spouse because we will have "better" times and we will certainly have "worse" times as well. But when the more difficult times come, how do we respond?

Sometimes the struggles appear around issues with the kids. Or they may be evident through interactions with our parents. Even more likely is that we will experience stress in some area of finances. When these occasions come, which they most certainly will, we too often find ourselves wanting to place blame. Since we certainly don't want to own responsibility, we are more likely to shove it over onto our spouse. Yet you have to ask yourself, "How effective does that prove to be?" Most of us would have to answer – "Not very effective at all. As a matter of fact it is usually destructive and builds walls between us."

When we find ourselves as couples experiencing these challenging times, we will fare much better if we will, together, forge ahead into the storms. Rather than trials coming between us and our spouse, they are truly opportunities that should push us closer together. If we are willing to team up with our spouse, it makes the storms much more "doable."

Purposeful Action: Identify one struggle in your life as a couple that is working to pull you apart. Talk with your husband or wife about the advantages, for both of you, of being on the same page. Look for common ground around the identified issue. And most importantly, commit to having each other's back.

Day 30

Want to Be Fixed?

Scripture – "How can you say to your brother, 'Let me take the speck out of your eye,' when all the time there is a plank in your own eye? You hypocrite, first take the plank out of your own eye, and then you will see clearly to remove the speck from your brother's eye." Matthew 7:4-5

When is the last time you went to your partner and said – "I am broken, please fix me?" Or, "I have some flaws, would you please correct them for me?" As you read these questions, you probably are thinking that I'm nuts (I may be but that is a different discussion for another time). Because my guess is that you have never made those statements.

Yet, I see many spouses approach their marital relationship as though God has shown up on their doorstep and given them some divine directive to fix their spouse. Ok, perhaps that is an overstatement. But, if we are honest, many of us have at one time or another believed that we knew the best way to do some particular thing and we saw it as our place to make the other person see it too. It may be something trivial, such as the best way to load the dishwasher or an issue that is a little more significant (though not much more) knowing the quickest route to take to the freeway. Whatever it might be, you may feel it is necessary to change their approach.

I sat last week with a premarital couple discussing personality trait differences. During the discussion about one particular trait of his which annoyed her, she said, "It's not a big deal. I just figure I can change him after we are married." If you have been married for any length of time, you know how naïve that statement is.

When we married, those vows came with an unspoken clause – "You know who I am, how I am, and the ways that I do things. Today, you are agreeing to accept me. Don't decide later on that you are going to change my shopping habits or the way that I drive the car. You agree today to accept me – faults blemishes and all."

Purposeful Action: I want to encourage you to find one trait in your spouse that can make you a little nuts because it so different from how you would do whatever it is. While this may be challenging, go to him or her, acknowledge the difference in style and say something like, "I want you to know that I realize our approach to this issue is very different. But mine is truly no more correct than yours. I am committing to you to do my best not to roll my eyes or discount your course of action and I want to respect, embrace, and support your way of doing things."

 *Day 31*

Remember the Good

Scripture – "I have not stopped giving thanks for
you, remembering you in my prayers."
Ephesians 1:16

Author Dana Reinhardt recounts the evening she
escorted her elderly grandmother to an event
honoring a Vietnam Vet. Complete with many
celebrities, Dana pointed several out to her, including
Robert Downey Jr. Later, exiting the facility, her
grandmother tripped and fell hard into the wheelchair
ramp, slicing her right shin. As she bled profusely, Robert
Downey Jr., came over and took charge of the situation –
comforting her grandmother, directing someone to call
for an ambulance, and another to bring her a glass of
water. He then took off his cream-colored linen jacket
and tied it around her wound. He stayed with her until
the ambulance came and held her hand until they left.

It wasn't until some years later, following his prison time
for some serious drug offenses that the author spotted
Robert Downey Jr. in a restaurant. She meekly went up to
him recounted the story, which he recalled, and said, "I
just want to thank you. And I wanted to tell you that it
was simply the kindest act I've ever witnessed." He stood
up, taking her hands, and said, "You have absolutely no
idea how much I needed to hear that today."

Over the course of your marriage or significant relationships, your partner has no doubt performed some extreme loving kind act toward you. For some, I realize that it may have been years ago and has since been buried under relational stress and tension. But just maybe, today is the day that your recollection and reminder of your gratefulness for their action is just what they "needed to hear."

Purposeful Action: Retrieve a fond memory from the archives of your mind today – something special, thoughtful, or generous that your spouse did for you. Be specific and thank him or her, telling them how much that meant to you. They will love you for it.

Day 32

Magnaflux

Scripture – "Not only so, but we also glory in our suffering, because we know that suffering produces perseverance; perseverance, character; and character, hope." Romans 5:3-4

I own a 1985 Firebird, having bought it in July of 1985. It has been a great car with lots of memories. However, after about 20 years and nearly 250,000 miles, it was time to park it and get something that made a little more sense to drive in Colorado, and so I did. The Firebird was tired, the engine no longer had the power it once had, and the transmission was slipping. I would drive it once in a while, but about 3 or 4 years ago – it really just sat parked. I knew that I would save my nickels and dimes and eventually begin to put it back into shape. A few months ago, I began to – by having a rebuilt engine and transmission put in it. Once again it came to life and was drivable. Yet, it just didn't seem to have the get up and go that it should have had and didn't run very smoothly. I drove it for all of 450 miles when the engine blew. Not what I expected after waiting all of this time. But the shop pulled out the engine and put another one in. Now it runs smoothly, with power, as it should. But what happened with the old engine that only lasted 450 miles? The engine manufacturer discovered that there was a crack in cylinder number 4. There is a process when rebuilding an engine that is called "magnaflux", a procedure where they use liquid and pressure to find any cracks, no matter how small. But somehow they had missed this one. As a result, the crack only got bigger and more exposed as the car was driven – until the engine would no longer perform.

Similarly, I see couples in my office who seem to be doing fairly well in their relationship, until pressures come: the kids are in trouble, there are financial concerns, or in-law issues – endless possibilities. However, here they sit – with their identified issue as to what they think the problem is – which is rarely the real issue. There are underlying cracks in the relationship (just like with the engine), that existed all the time, but were not visible until the pressures came. The pressures simply exposed the cracks, exposed the problems that were there all along – the miscommunications, the lack of attention to the relationship, self-centeredness, unkindness, etc.

In the magnafluxing process, the pressure is supposed to reveal the cracks so that appropriate steps can be taken to avoid the very problem I experienced. Pressures in our marriages and relationships can serve the same purpose. They can be an opportunity to reveal areas of weakness so that we know better where to focus our efforts and attention to improve our relationships. As you experience pressures, remember, pressures are not the problem. But they will expose the areas that are - that need your focus.

Purposeful Action: Identify one of the unintended fractures that exists in your relationship. Communicate your awareness of this particular issue to your mate along with your gratefulness for the opportunity that it provides to repair it. Letting your spouse know that you desire to resolve issues can be deeply reassuring.

 *Day 33*

Ledger Book Thinking

Scripture – "Do nothing out of selfish ambition or vain conceit, but in humility consider others better than ourselves." Philippians 2:3

"I met one woman in Georgia who has been married to her husband for over 60 years. After being asked for her best relationship advice, she paused and then said, 'Don't be afraid to be the one who loves most." – Nate Bagley

I thought about this advice as I sat this week with a couple whose relationship has been fractured. The wife has been deeply wounded emotionally by her husband. While her husband intellectually understands that, he is having difficulty at a heart level. As a result, he is frustrated that she can't just accept his apology and jump fully back into the marriage game.

As I spent some time with just him, I encouraged him to go above and beyond in his pursuit of his wife's heart. However, he kept wanting to make this fair. In other words, if he was going to make efforts then she needed to as well. If he were to try to listen and be more open, then it is only appropriate that she invest at the same level. This is what I would call "ledger book thinking." For example, if he pays her two compliments today, then she needs to also offer two compliments.

While I acknowledge that it would be great if they were both able to emotionally give equally to the relationship – that is not possible right now. The most powerful weapon at his disposal to break this stalemate is to genuinely love his wife. He seems so afraid, feeling that if they are not loving evenly then he will somehow be taken advantage of. However, I would submit that if he will stop being afraid of loving most, and instead genuinely give of himself to her without keeping track – the logjam has a much greater chance of breaking loose.

Purposeful Action: When you find yourself feeling that things are not equal or fair, do what is counter intuitive, and love even more. If you feel it is not fair that you have cleaned up the kitchen the last three evenings, clean it again. If your mate is busy but it is his or her turn to help the kids with their homework, embrace the opportunity to assist the kids. In the words of the woman from Georgia – "Don't be afraid to be the one who loves most." What a great mantra.

 *Day 34*

Love Me like the Dog

Scripture – "I am my beloved's and my beloved is mine." Song of Solomon 6:3a

During this past week, I sat in my office with a couple who was definitely experiencing some disconnection issues. As the husband expressed his frustration regarding how his wife was treating him, he said, "I just wish you would treat me as good as you do the dog. I would be happy if you would simply love me as much as you do her." Wow! What a statement. Yet, I wonder how many of us have felt similarly?

A survey by the American Veterinary Medical Association in 2013 reported that singles (especially men) are increasingly turning to their pets for love and for a sense of family. The release went on to state that pet ownership by all singles, including those who have never been married as well as those who are separated or divorced, jumped 16.6% from 2006 to 2011.

It is easy to understand this because pets are terrific company for those who are alone. Pets can be wonderful companions who love us unconditionally. Yet, they are not meant to be substitutes for people – for human contact. And this is especially true if we are married.

I know that there are many individuals, like the one

above, who feel as though their spouse loves the family dog more than they love them. Please understand that loving the animal isn't the problem. I love my dogs Jolee and Bailey dearly, and yes, they are a part of the family. But they could <u>never</u> be a replacement for my wife. When a spouse makes a statement like the one above, it is a thermometer reading that says – "We are not connected as partners and I desperately want to be."

Purposeful Action: Do you show more love and care and attention for your spouse than you do the family dog (or cat or any other pet)? If you aren't sure – I encourage you to do a self-check today. Try this – every time you start to reach for the pet or say something to them, first reach for your spouse and express your love and affection for them. This may be quite revealing – and rewarding.

Day 35

What?

Scripture – "A good man brings good things out of the good stored up in his heart, and an evil man brings evil things out of the evil stored up in his heart. For the mouth speaks what the heart is full of." Luke 6:45

As a child, I used to hear my parents speak a language that kept us kids from understanding them. It worked pretty well until we got a little older and could figure it out. You see, it wasn't a real language but a made up one called "Double Talk." As an adult, I can't begin to tell you the rules of this made up language, but I can speak it, and I used it when my children were young and I didn't want them to know what I was saying. When they would hear this, they were left confused and bewildered. Sometimes, as married couples, we may not speak in this made up language, but we engage in communication that can be just as difficult to understand.

"What's the matter?" "Nothing" (followed by an obvious look that all is not well).

"Where would you like to go to dinner?" "Wherever you would like. Anyplace is fine." "Well then how about the Italian place over on the north side?" "I guess that would be ok" (said with a less than enthusiastic tone and a look of obvious displeasure).

These situations can lead to frustration and confusion when one person engages in "Double Talk." In marriage, "Double Talk" is saying one thing when you mean another. Or you may say one thing verbally while your non-verbal language is communicating something far different. Confusion is the result. Yet, you frequently expect your spouse to know what you are saying and you may even find yourself upset when they try to guess what you mean and they get it wrong.

In order to foster healthy communication and solid conflict resolution, it is essential that we not talk, figuratively, out of both sides of our mouth. Communication is challenging enough without complicating it with unclear mixed messages.

Double talk is fun when it is a made up language but is highly frustrating when you want to understand and be on the same page as your partner.

Purposeful Action: Ask your husband or wife if there are times when they feel that you are not saying what you mean, when, perhaps, your words do not match your body language. Have them give you a specific example. Without getting defensive, explore ways that you can become more consistent and emotionally honest in your communication.

Day 36

Connected Couples

Scripture – "I appeal to you, brothers and sisters, in the name of our Lord Jesus Christ, that all of you agree with one another in what you say and that there be no divisions among you, but that you be perfectly united in mind and thought." I Corinthians 1:10

Conflict, fights, arguments, disagreements – these are all words that make us want to go hide. As I sit with couples on a daily basis, I listen to the creative ways that each party escapes in order to avoid all of those above words. While there may be something that is bothering them, they will avoid discussing it for fear that it will lead to an "argument." When he or she comes home in the evening, their ultimate goal is not to spend time together or emotionally connect but to just "avoid a fight." It almost at times feels like when we were teenagers and our goal was just to stay out of trouble. While it is nice to have a quiet evening and not experience conflict – that position by itself is a long ways from intimacy and connection.

In a study conducted by the University of California, researchers examined how couples fought. They made an interesting discovery regarding those couples who fought, but did so productively without being adversarial, and who actually increased their connectedness. What was the secret? It is so simple that we might be tempted to just dismiss it as semantics. But I would remind you that the difference it made for these couples was powerful.

Here you go – they simply changed the pronouns that they used. Instead of using words like "I," "me," or "mine," they used the plurals "we," "us," and "ours." Really? Really! Why would that small change in words have such an impact? Because instead of creating a feeling of "me against you," it indicated that we are in this together, working to jointly find a solution. It communicates that we are on the same team.

Recall when you first entered the relationship with your significant other – you were looking for someone to be "on your team." Team mates will absolutely encounter differences – but they are still on the same side.

Purposeful Action: The next time that you find yourself in a conflict with your significant other, notice the words that you use in your conversation. Do you tend to use words that talk about yourself or do you choose language that reflects the fact that the two of you are on the same team? Look for ways to build a foundation of "we" through the words that you use.

Day 37

Is that Funny?

Scripture – "The cheerful heart has a continual feast." Proverbs 15:15b

"There's a conversation between a minister, a priest, and a rabbi . . . . . " Ok, no I am not going to tell a joke, but if I did, would you laugh? Well, maybe that's not a fair question because people are more likely to groan at my jokes than laugh (unless of course they are really smart ☺), because I love puns. The more punny, the better.

I raise this issue because I see more and more couples that are serious. Of course there are times to be serious. I mean that I see people who are serious all the time. They grit their teeth, furrow their brow, and intensely approach their relationships as though every move and every decision is a life or death issue. Whether they are watching a sitcom or their favorite sports team play – there is no levity.

Life is serious. We were placed on this planet for a purpose by our Creator and that is a serious matter. However, how we live this life can be absolutely full of humor. Even in scripture, as I read the history of the Hebrew people or the words of Jesus to the crowds of people, God's sense of humor peaks through. While life may be serious, we don't have to take ourselves so seriously.

I find opportunities every day to laugh at myself. Whether I hit my head on something, which my kids will tell you I am a master at, or whether I say something absolutely goofy, it is an opportunity to laugh. I have known people to fall out of bed during sex, and chuckle whenever they think about it.

Purposeful Action: Humor makes the seriousness of life more bearable. So, be intentional about laughing today. The only rule is, it can't be laughing at your spouse. You can laugh at yourself, you can laugh at a sitcom, or you can laugh at the dog. And if you can't seem to find something funny in the trivialities of the day, find a joke to tell your spouse. Don't have a joke – google the internet for one. No excuses – laugh with your mate today.

 *Day 38*

Anchors

Scripture – "Remember the days of old; consider the generations long past. Ask your father and he will tell you, your elders, and they will explain to you."
Deuteronomy 32:7

What are your anchors? Huh? What are your anchors? Now you may be thinking, "Hmm, what weighs me down? Well there are certainly the bills, the job, holiday dinners at the in-laws, and those annoying parent-teacher conferences at the kid's school." But I am not talking about heavy things from which you feel there is no escape. I am talking about the things that keep you grounded – particularly in your important relationships.

If I were to ask you to itemize the 5 to 10 most grounding memorable events of your marriage, could you do it? What would be on the list – the day he proposed, a particular birthday celebration, a milestone anniversary, when you made your first scary but significant financial decision together, when he or she came to a special work function that honored your sacrifice and service, or another event around which memories have been built? All healthy relationships have some of these but oftentimes we get so weighed down with the cares of life that we fail to anchor and remember the things that are important. Or sadder yet would be if you have failed to create those important moment in the first place.

Purposeful Action: Make it a point to stop and remember your important anchors – you may do that by looking at vacation photos, watching videos of the kids together or by sharing stories with friends. If you are one who hasn't created memorable moments, it is never too late to start. But it will require intentionality. Set as your goal a plan and carry out something truly special with your spouse that will create a pleasant anchoring memory.

()

Day 39

What's the Value?

Scripture – "Don't have anything to do with foolish and stupid arguments, because you know they produce quarrels. And the Lord's servant must not be quarrelsome but must be kind to everyone . . . " 2 Timothy 2:23-24a

I learned an important lesson last week. We were cleaning out some things from our downstairs and had put in a pick-up call to Goodwill. As my wife was giving them a list regarding any larger items, which included two TVs, she discovered that they don't accept TVs anymore. She assured them that they are in perfect working condition. Nope, they don't take them. She thought that surely someone would – nope – not Salvation Army, not Disabled Veterans, not anyone.

Now you may be thinking – "Ok, so what's the big deal?" Well, one of the TVs, while it is big and very heavy, unlike the light weight flat-screens of today, cost over $1,000 twenty plus years ago. But now it is worth nothing? Did I mention that it works as well as when it was new? Yet, no one will take it. But we did discover that Best Buy will accept it for recycling . . . if we pay them $25. Nothing like adding insult to injury.

It is one thing to put too much stock and value in a silly TV. But I have even seen couples who would have a "no holds barred" battle over which TV to purchase in the first place. They might be inclined to verbally and emotionally take each other out at the knees for something that in a few years is worthless. Or how often do we overemphasize our position in an argument with our spouse? Winning the argument takes precedence over communicating love; getting our way is more important than being kind.

The question we have to ask ourselves is, "What has lasting value?" Is it the battle over where we go on vacation or is it the heart and soul of the one with whom we are vacationing?" We probably know the answer.

Purposeful Action: Communicate value to your mate today. You can do this in some small way, such as – leaving a sticky note on the bathroom mirror, texting them during the work day, or bringing home their favorite cookie from the store. You are letting them know that you are thinking about them. And that communicates value.

Day 40

Do You See?

Scripture – "Not looking to your own interests but each of you to the interests of the others."
Philippians 2:4

While people's inclinations seem to be the same from generation to generation, the nuances of the differences in issues can vary. One of those issues that has changed faster than our relational insights, has been around technology – particularly cell phones. I can assure you that 20 years ago I was not dealing with this in marriage counseling - at all, while today there is not a week, and sometimes, not even a day that goes by that it doesn't come up.

A prime example of this occurred in my office yesterday. The wife was in tears as she related how once again she was playing second fiddle in the marital orchestra. She had arrived home in emotional turmoil at the dismissive manner with which she was being treated at work. While her husband isn't always the greatest listener, she was in need of a safe place to talk about the situation and she figured he would be supportive.

About 10 minutes into the conversation, he reaches for his cell phone that had buzzed and began to respond to a text he had received. She was flabbergasted and said to him, "I am not finished talking about this." He didn't respond because he didn't even hear her. He was now caught up in his texting conversation. She dejectedly walked away and he didn't even see what he had carelessly, and dismissively, done. Whether he meant to or not, he had just communicated to his wife that she was not as important to him as whoever was on the other end of the phone conversation.

We often don't see what being tethered to a virtual world does to the real flesh and blood people standing right in front of us. And when we miss that, our most important relationships suffer.

Purposeful Action: So, today's tip is simple: put the phone away! You do not need it attached to you every moment. Perhaps you need to put into place some phone free zones or times so that you can actually engage in relationships without distraction. Try it. I promise – the addiction shakes will stop after a while. And if they don't, maybe your spouse, who is in front of you, will speak to you with "LOL" "BTW" and ☺ until they do.

Day 41

How's Your Thermostat?

Scripture – "But the fruit of the Spirit is love, joy, peace, forbearance, kindness, goodness, faithfulness, gentleness and self-control. Against such things there is no law." Galatians 5:22-23

Now I can imagine that you are wondering what in the world thermostats have to do with your marriage or relationship. You may be thinking that perhaps I am going to talk about the temperature gauge of your relationships or something like that. But actually, it is going to be different than you may think.

Recently, while carrying a load of laundry through the hallway, I reached over to adjust the thermostat on the heat/AC. When I touched it, static electricity from my finger hit the thermostat and fried the digital readout. I tried putting in new batteries and some other creative ideas, but nothing would fix it. Ultimately, I had to go buy a new thermostat. As I shared my story with the sales associate at Home Depot, he said, "Your static shock that morning is not what blew out the thermostat." Surprised, I said "It's not?" He replied, "No, it is the fact that you have probably static shocked that a hundred times. Each time, it builds up in the system until finally your most recent one was what pushed it over the functional edge."

Many times I sit with clients in my office and hear about

the latest crisis that has sent them over the edge. It may be a major contention or, more frequently, something that, to the outside observer, seems so trivial. And yet, what transpires with this couple is what happened to my thermostat. It wasn't the single unkind word or demeaning comment that brought them to the edge of splitting. It was the fact that unkind words of this nature had been uttered hundreds of times before. This was just the one that finally blew out their ability to hold it together. Rather than allow your negative words and sometimes toxic treatment of your spouse to build up over time to an explosive point, I want to encourage you to distress the situation instead.

Purposeful Action: Watch your mate's face today to get a read on how their thermostat is doing. Perhaps you carelessly make that cutting remark that you have uttered dozens of times. If you are watching the body language, you are likely to see when you have shocked their thermostat again. Quickly own your mistake, apologize, and endeavor to correct the behavior.

Day 42

A Kiss a day . . . . .

Scripture – "Let him kiss me with the kisses of his mouth—for your love is more delightful than wine." Song of Solomon 1:2

Can a kiss a day keep the doctor away? Wow – wouldn't that be great! If that were the case, if kissing could be both fun and healthy, how cool would that be? In a recent interview, Andrea Demirjian, author of "Kissing: Everything You Ever Wanted to Know about One of Life's Sweetest Pleasures," offered eight reasons why she thinks this just might be the case. I want to share these eight benefits with you.

1) Kissing reduces your blood pressure. It helps dilate your blood vessels which may lead to lower pressure.
2) It can relieve cramps and headaches. The reason for this is similar to the one above.
3) Kissing can fight cavities. It can produce saliva which washes away plaque. I know, not too romantic, but practical.
4) You may feel happier. Kissing can cause the release of neurotransmitters in the brain that lead to feelings of happiness, satisfaction, and even bonding.
5) Kissing can burn calories. A vigorous kiss may burn 8 to 16 calories.

6) Your self-esteem may be boosted. Higher incomes were earned by the men in a study who received a passionate kiss from their wives before leaving for work. Just think — if you want your spouse to earn more money, maybe a morning kiss is the trick.
7) Kissing can tone your facial muscles.
8) If you are not married but are searching, kissing has been shown to be a measure of compatibility.

A separate study found that in a six week period, those who increased their kissing time by a mere 15 minutes displayed lower cholesterol readings, reduced stress, and an overall improvement in their relationship quality. Conversely, those who didn't increase time kissing had elevated levels of the stress hormone cortisol.

So, what's the tip? Kind of a no-brainer actually. Kiss your mate more and in turn experience better health, lower stress, and an improved relationship. Now who wouldn't want those benefits? The best parts are — it's fun, it's free, and it's easy.

Purposeful Action: So, try this simple exercise — finish reading this and go kiss your spouse. If it has been a while since you have done that, they may be in shock. That's OK. One kiss today might be just what is needed. But as time goes on, I hope you will repeat as often as possible for maximum benefit.

Day 43

Hanging Out

Scripture – "The LORD God said, 'It is not good for the man to be alone. I will make a helper suitable for him.' the man said, 'This is now bone of my bones and flesh of my flesh;
she shall be called 'woman,' for she was taken out of man.' That is why a man leaves his father and mother and is united to his wife, and they become one flesh." Genesis 2:18; 23-24

"I just say, 'Yes Dear,'" was his response. Of course, you are wondering what the question was.

We were recently privileged to attend the anniversary party for a couple who have been married 65 years. Wow – that is longer than I have been alive (though not by much). At 88 and 85, Elinor and Archie could easily pass for 10 years younger than they are. As a matter of fact, Elinor had even made some of the food for the reception spread.

Family and friends had gathered for this memorable occasion to honor the anniversary couple. Yet, as I looked around the room, it was hard not to notice many couples who, though married for significantly shorter periods of time, seemed much less happy. Several were sitting across the room from their respective spouses, seemingly uninterested in engaging with them.

But this was not true of Elinor and Archie. As I visited with them, always wanting to glean wisdom from seasoned couples, I asked the question, "What is the secret to the longevity of your marriage." That was when Archie responded with the quote that I began with. While that seemed a safe and humorous response – I couldn't let it go at that. So I pressed for more.

Then they both chimed in saying that even though they had normal ups and downs and challenging times, they had made it a point of doing life together. They learned that by being intentional about this, they had developed a real affinity for one another. Simply stated – they just like hanging out together. And the longer they are together, the more they enjoy one another's company.

While this may sound simplistic, know that no one gets to 65 years without some obstacles to overcome. Even so, they successfully found that committing to "do life together" made a huge difference in the enjoyment of the journey.

Purposeful Action: Identify the three most significant ways that you and your spouse have managed to "do life together" over the course of your marriage. Are those still relevant? If so, super! But if not, invite your husband or wife to share with you things that would contribute to a desire to hang out with you more. Pay close attention, without resistance, and commit yourself to learning to "do life together" again.

Day 44

Do Something Different

Scripture – "Above all, love each other deeply, because love covers over a multitude of sins." I Peter 4:8

We all get into routines. Sometimes they are good ones – like brushing your teeth. Other times, not so good, such as yelling when you are frustrated. As a result, there are certainly those routines that we want to hang on to while others we need to jettison as quickly as possible.

For example, a couple sat in my office yesterday discussing a blow-up they had last weekend. It seems that when the wife comes home tired from work, she occasionally forgets to close the garage door. Since this happens with some frequency, the husband has been known to respond with harsh criticism. As you can imagine, the conversation gets intense, voice are raised, feelings are hurt, and tears may be shed. Ultimately, the couple spends the evening in separate rooms of the house licking their wounds, both feeling disrespected and unloved.

Now one would think that after this scenario is repeated a couple of times, the husband would try a different approach. But invariably he defaults back to the harsh criticism. We can easily find ourselves living with the person in our head (our thoughts and perceptions of our spouse) rather than the person standing in front of us. If this is going to change, we need to break the dysfunctional pattern of interaction.

So, just to stimulate your creative thinking, let me tell you what happened with the couple above. One day the husband came home to find the garage door opened again. But this time rather than walk in loaded for bear, he came in found his wife – passionately embraced her and said, "Thank you for loving me and anticipating my return by opening the garage for me. That was incredibly kind." She was stunned – pleasantly so. Two things happened: 1) they had a wonderfully different evening together, and 2) his kindness was a motivator for her to be a little more diligent about taking care of the garage door.

Purposeful Action: When confronted with one of those unpleasant and frequent interactions, pause and ask yourself, "What can I do differently this time that could break the pattern?" Responding in a new way, will speak to him or her of your love and care. It can also demonstrate that in a concrete manner.

Day 45

Protecting Against Infidelity

Scripture – "Your word is a lamp for my feet, a light on my path." Psalm 119:105

I sit with couples on a regular basis who have been impacted by infidelity. And I am not talking only about a physical affair. While unfaithfulness can certainly be sexual, it can just as easily be emotional. It can be engaged in online or in person. A large majority of divorce proceedings cite Facebook connections as a contributor to divorces.

So, what can we do to prevent individuals from straying outside of the boundaries of their marriages? Should we constantly monitor each other's email and Facebook accounts? Should we sneak around, hiding behind bushes and spy on each other? While those are certainly possibilities, I am not sure that they are the best or most healthy approaches.

Maybe there is a better strategy. Author Dr. Tim Clinton recently reported that couples who read the Bible together are profoundly impacted. He says that "research shows that if you engage in [reading] Scripture at least four days each week, it will change your choices, your relationship with your spouse, and lowers the risk for infidelity by 60%." I find that research to be powerful and encouraging. Think about it – if a medical journal reported on a new pill that when taken would have that kind of influence on your marriage, wouldn't you be inclined to run out to Walgreens and get the prescription filled tonight? Most of us probably would. But what Dr. Clinton has shared is even easier – if we will make it a priority by carving out the time to do it.

It seems so simple – reading the Bible significantly reduces the risk of infidelity because it helps us to continually dip our bucket in the well of God's truth. And in doing so – it changes us! If I really want to build a hedge of protection around my marriage, allowing God to change who I am is a much more powerful strategy than monitoring my spouse's online accounts.

Purposeful Action: Do you want to be changed? Do you want your marriage to be changed? Discuss with your mate the benefits of reading scripture together. Then make a plan – where in the Bible you would want to start, the best time of day or week to read together, and who will initiate at any given time. Commit to do this for at least three months and then re-evaluate to discover any impact that this is having on your relationship.

 *Day 46*

Responding to Crisis

Scripture – "Therefore everyone who hears these words of mine and puts them into practice is like a wise man who built his house on the rock. The rain came down, the streams rose, and the winds blew and beat against that house; yet it did not fall, because it had its foundation on the rock. But everyone who hears these words of mine and does not put them into practice is like a foolish man who built his house on sand. The rain came down, the streams rose, and the winds blew and beat against that house, and it fell with a great crash." Matthew 7:24-27

On July 6, 2013, Asiana Airlines Flight 214 from South Korea crashed short of the runway at San Francisco Airport. The plane struck the ground with the tail hitting a seawall. Three flight attendants were ejected. One of the remaining flight attendants, Lee Yoon-Hye, helped hundreds of passengers get safely out of the plane and onto the runway.

When an emergency slide deployed improperly, Lee handed a knife to the co-pilot who punctured the slide. When she saw flames erupt, she tossed a fire extinguisher to a colleague. It was later discovered that she did all of this with a broken tailbone.

You may be thinking, "Ok, a heroic story, but how does that relate to me?" Here is the point: Lee was able to perform at this level in a crisis, in part, because their flight training is intense. They practice and practice evacuating a plane until they are able to empty a jumbo jet filled with passengers in 90 seconds. Then when a real crisis happens, as it did on that flight, they just follow their training.

Wouldn't it be nice if we were able to similarly respond to crises in our significant relationships with that kind of deftness? Instead, many couples hit a stressful situation and implode or have some kind of meltdown. Rather than work as a team, as Lee and her colleagues did, it's easy for us to turn on each other.

Purposeful Action: What if we practiced? What if when times are good we had honest conversations about crises that we are likely to face? I want to suggest two things for you to do towards better preparing you as a couple for times that are likely to be challenging: 1) Find a book about strengthening marriages and read it and talk about it together, and 2) Locate a marriage retreat, couple's workshop that you could attend or even a webinar that you could watch as a couple. Preparing for the unknown is one of the best protective strategies that you put in place to protect your marriage.

.

 *Day 47*

Who Do You Live With?

Scripture – "Let your conversation be always full of grace, seasoned with salt, so that you may know how to answer everyone." Colossians 4:6

"Well," you think, "I live with my spouse," or "my spouse and our kids." While that is certainly true but I'm looking a little deeper. You see, when we get married we typically feel that we are marrying the ideal person. However, as the months and years go by, we may begin to find them, well . . . less than ideal. For example, when he would occasionally leave his dirty clothes on the floor, you initially may have thought it cute. But over time, it has become his way of making work for you or just trying to tick you off. Or at least, so you believe.

I find great truth in a statement by a family therapist named John Van Epp; "You don't really live with the partner in your home, you live with the partner in your head." Think about that for a moment using the dirty clothes example. How did the husband's leaving of dirty clothes on the floor progress from cute to fight inducing? While it is possible that his intent has changed, it is far more likely that our perception of his intent has changed. With that shift we begin to see a boogey man around every corner. In other words, we question his or her intent and motivation about virtually everything.

Irritating and annoying behaviors are a natural part of nearly every relationship. It is a two-way street. But the good news is – things can change. The challenging news it that change begins with you. You see no matter how frustrating your partner's behavior is, what often makes it so frustrating is your interpretation of it. We attach meaning to behavior – and sometimes we completely miss the mark.

Purposeful Action: I want to encourage you to try something today. As you notice one of your mate's annoying behaviors, ask yourself this question: "Is it possible that what he or she is doing right now is in no way aimed at me?" And if it is not, how does that alter your feelings? Actively look for ways to love the person in front of you, not the one inside your head.

 *Day 48*

The Silent Treatment

Scripture – "Be kind and compassionate to one another, forgiving each other, just as in Christ God forgave you." Ephesians 4:32

You call your husband during the day to let him know that you are upset with the fact that he forgot to take the trash to the street this morning, before he left for work, as he had promised. Not a big deal in and of itself – but it is about to become one. Instead of accepting the responsibility and expressing regret, he mumbles something that simply allows him to get off the phone. You don't think much about it.

But later, when he gets home from work, he seems distant. You try your best to make conversation but it is met with stonewalling. He seems to be busy doing things that allow him to avoid you. As you pursue him with questions, you are met with one-word responses. What is happening? You are being given the "silent treatment."

We have all been guilty at one time or another of giving someone the cold shoulder. But why? Usually because we feel hurt and powerless. This is our way of reclaiming some kind of control. But as one therapist stated, it is the "equivalent of a deadly emotional assassination." The reason it is so deadly is that it thwarts the purpose of our anger or frustration. When we are upset we can use the opportunity for constructive communication that can bring about positive change. But when we punish our mate with the "silent treatment," we create an adversarial relationship.

Instead of resorting to this punishing and relationship killing technique, I want to urge you to use some self-talk to stay in the conversation. Make a commitment to your spouse to not withdraw when feelings are bruised or talking is difficult. While you may need to agree to revisit the issue later when feelings are more settled, commit yourself to following through with this action. Bottom line – while it can be a hard pattern to break, it is imperative that you do so for the sake of your marriage. Cold shoulders can kill connection while embracing the opportunity for honest dialog can build renewed vibrancy.

Purposeful Action: The next time your husband or wife points out one of your short-comings (I'm sure you have at least one), take notice of your immediate feelings. If you find yourself wanting to withdraw to lick your wounds – stop! Instead, listen carefully to see if what they said possible has merit. If it does, be quick to respond with both humility and attentiveness to your mate's needs.

Day 49

Seize the Opportunity

Scripture – "Rejoice with those who rejoice; mourn with those who mourn." Romans 12:15

It has been a long and somewhat frustrating day at work. You arrive home planning to have a little solace in the front of the TV. However, as you walk in the door, your spouse, who is bubbling with excitement wants to talk. Talk – ugh – this requires thinking and brain cells that are functioning on impulse power only. Still she wants to tell you about a co-worker she helped to think through and solve a problem on her own today. You listen with half of one ear and then make a flippant comment, something like – "Yea that's good, but your co-worker will probably go back and screw it up again tomorrow." And with that one statement, you could feel the air escape the room.

A researcher at the University of California, Santa Barbara discovered that a strong predictor of marital satisfaction is how well the couple is able to celebrate each other's positive events. These couples are much more successful than those who commiserate over the negatives. This study found that couples experiencing the greatest relationship satisfaction where those who responded enthusiastically to each other's successes, ask questions, gave compliments, and were each other's biggest cheerleaders.

Now if you're like me, there is nothing very surprising in this report. It makes perfect sense actually. However, here is the astonishing part – we acknowledge the truth of this research but then continue to plop down on the couch in front of the TV, computer, or video game without giving our spouse the attention he or she desires and deserves.

Purposeful Action: Would you like to improve your marriage today, even just a little? Then seize the opportunity – whether big or small – to affirm and celebrate with your spouse. If she tells you about a positive or productive conversation she had with one of the kids, affirm the value and optimism of that interaction. If he relates a solution he figured out to avert a brewing conflict at work, verbally support his resourcefulness. Celebrate each other's victories.

 *Day 50*

Are You Ready?

Scripture – "Consider it pure joy, my brothers and sisters, whenever you face trials of many kinds, because you know that the testing of your faith produces perseverance. Let perseverance finish its work so that you may be mature and complete, not lacking anything." James 1:2-4

I recently came across the following quote, "Marriage is your last best chance to grow up." Now, before I go any further, I really want you to let that sink in. So (with Jeopardy music playing in the background), ponder for a moment those words. Ok – "I'll take growing up for $400."

Many of us may think that "growing up" was what we did in our teens or maybe even our 20's. But I would offer for your consideration, that maybe it is after we get married that we truly enter a season with our best chance for growing up.

Think about it – when do you act the most childish – demanding (or at least expecting) to have things the way that you want them. And if you don't get them, the tantrums follow. Ok, maybe you don't flail on the floor kicking and screaming like you did when you were a kid (or maybe you do), but you probably know how to pout, give the "cold shoulder," and punish using silence with the best of them. Some might say, "Well, you don't understand. He (or she) brings out the worst in me." Maybe – but in that is the best opportunity to grow.

With pretentious behavior, it is easy to convince others that we have it all together, at least for a while. And for as long as we are able to pull that off, no growth on our part is required. But our partner – now that is another matter. He or she knows us – faults, goofiness, absurdities, and all. We can't fool them. But we can choose to grow.

Not growing up is easy. Growing up though takes intentional effort. As spouses, we and they can provide loving caring reflection – if we are willing to allow each other to do that. And if we are, this really might be our best chance to grow up. I encourage you to engage authentically with your spouse today, owning your own stuff while forgiving them for theirs.

Purposeful Action: The next time your partner says something to you that causes you to bristle, and you find yourself thinking, "That's it – I have had it. I want to take my toys and go home;" hit the pause button. This is a red flag that just might be an indicator that this is a potential area of growth for you. Instead of sulking, why not try pondering what has been said with an open, non-defensive posture? This honest look inward can lead to growth for you as an individual as well as increased connection as a couple.

 *Day 51*

What Does Your Conversation Communicate?

Scripture – "Reckless words pierce like a sword, but the tongue of the wise brings healing." Proverbs 12:18

"There are just two things I'd need to find out everything I want to know about everyone: 1) Let me see them drive; 2) Let me hear them talk about marriage . . . . That's going to tell me exactly your relationship to the world." – Jerry Seinfeld

Most of us would probably agree with the first part of that statement – that is as long as we are talking about the other person's driving habits and not our own. However, we probably haven't thought about the second part of the quote in the same terms. Yet, there is great truth in what he said.

If someone were to overhear you talk about your marriage, would they hear stories of loyalty and love, sacrifice and treasuring, or disgruntled complaints, put downs, and animosity? Because how you talk about your relationship with your spouse indicates how you will operate in relation to your boss, colleagues, and even trusted friends. If you will speak disparagingly about the most important relationship in your life, what will you say regarding the rest of us?

At the same time, if your conversation about your marriage is laced with phrases of acknowledgement, praise, understanding, valuing, and building up – you are much more likely to relate to the rest of your world similarly. Speech that is treasuring in nature is an indication of behavior that reflects those same values.

Purposeful Action: Pay close attention to the words you speak about your marriage and your spouse. If you catch yourself using words of disgust or words that tear down, whether you are talking to your spouse or someone else – stop talking. Remember, while they may reflect your feelings about that relationship, they also speak volumes about you and how you relate to your world. As the proverb says, rather than using reckless words, look for the things that you can say that build others up and bring healing – especially when it relates to your spouse.

 *Day 52*

Are You Absently Present?

Scripture – "Therefore if you have any encouragement from being united with Christ, if any comfort from his love, if any common sharing in the Spirit, if any tenderness and compassion, then make my joy complete by being like-minded, having the same love, being one in spirit and of one mind."
Philippians 2:1-2

In 2016 *Psychology Today* called attention to the fact that smartphones fragment human consciousness. They contend that the habitual use of smartphones lowers our ability to be empathetic as well as diminishes the "quality of conversation."

Today I want to discuss some unintended by-products of our smartphones. The above report went on to state that when cell phones are present, "people have the constant urge to seek out information, check for communication, and direct their thoughts to other people and worlds." As this happens, people begin to feel that, even though you might be physically present, you are emotionally absent. The result is a decreased likelihood that the other person will self-disclose.

Relationship researcher John Gottman talks about the importance of the rhythms of interaction. Couples have unstructured moments, in each other's company, when their attention is not drawn somewhere else, that naturally produce spontaneous interactions, laughter, and unexpected, yet significant, connections. These are the "hallmarks of satisfying relationships." There is a real danger that, whether riding in the car or watching TV with our mate, the constant presence of our smartphone may cause us to miss important opportunities for connection.

Purposeful Action: Be more intentional in creating space that allows for the kind of interactions and responses which grow out of the natural ebb and flow of uninterrupted relationship. In other words – when you are present with your spouse – really be "present!" Arrange an evening with your spouse, whether you go out or designate some time at home, when you do not have your smartphone with you. If you are out for dinner, leave the phone in the car or at home. If you are at home, leave the phone in another room out of earshot. If your hands are starting to sweat as you contemplate this, rest assured, you will survive. And better still, your relationship will be given the priority that can lead to greater depth and connectivity.

Day 53

How to Soften Your Arguments

Scripture – "Let us therefore make every effort to do what leads to peace and to mutual edification."
Romans 14:19

Bret was working out in the garage when Susan came out to discuss a sticky situation with him regarding one of the children. She knew that they had different perspectives on the situation and would probably disagree on how best to handle this. As they talked (actually – argued), Bret could feel his blood pressure rising and Susan sensed the tension increasing. After a few minutes, they decided to go sit in the living room to finish their discussion. Surprisingly, while sitting on the couch they were able to get on the same page in pretty short order. Why did that make a difference?

A recent study that came out of MIT, Harvard, and Yale showed "that people are more flexible and accommodating when they sit on cushioned surfaces." Hmm – "Well that is easy," you might think. "We will just sit on the couch from now on and all of our arguments will be settled." Ok – it might not be that easy. But think about it – when you are sitting on a hard surface, you may find yourself getting uncomfortable and anxious to end the discussion. This may lead to short and even irritated responses. While sitting on a cushioned surface allows you to feel more comfortable and not in as much of a hurry. Out of that can result a more productive discussion.

As I reflected on this study, I was reminded that my wife recently purchased cushions for the wooden chairs in our dining room. We had some friends over for dinner a few weeks ago and wound up spending the entire evening in the dining room rather than moving into the living room, which would have probably been our normal pattern. We had a great time and there is no doubt in my mind that the new cushions made the difference.

Purposeful Action: While cushions do not solve arguments, if the chance of being able to work together is even slightly increased by sitting on the couch, it is worth a try. The next time you find yourself engaged in a significant discussion with your spouse (whether it's about the kids, finances, parents, or work issues), try sitting in a more comfortable setting. See if that might help create a more relaxed, less rushed, and productive conversation.

Day 54

Defend, Defend, Defend . . . Or

Scripture – "Whoever conceals their sins does not prosper, but the one who confesses and renounces them finds mercy." Proverbs 28:13

D o you remember when you were young and your mother said something like, "Don't eat any cookies before dinner or you will ruin your appetite." So what did you do? For me, the call of the cookies was oftentimes too strong and I would succumb. But then you know what would happen. I wasn't hungry and then would come the lecture. Oh how I hated the lecture. So, I would defend my actions saying something along the lines of, "Well you said dinner was going to be later," or "That's not fair. You let _____ (fill in the blank of a sibling's name) have cookies yesterday." We can be very creative in our defensive comebacks. However, have you noticed that the more you defend, the more exasperated the other person becomes?

I love the TV show NCIS. Leroy Jethro Gibbs, who is the boss of the investigative team, frequently says, "Never say you're sorry. It is a sign of weakness." As much as I wouldn't want to disagree with Gibbs to his face, in this post I will. He couldn't be more wrong.

When I make poor choices, but then defend them to my spouse – I erode the foundation of trust and intimacy that exist between us. But when I confess my mistake and apologize – sincerely – I open the door to possibilities. Possibilities for openness, healing, and a renewed level of intimacy. Confession tears down walls and builds bridges.

Purposeful Action: So, when you misstep today, rather than get in your mate's face with your attempts at deflection and defense – try confession, apology, and owning your mistake. The age old quote that "Confession is good for the soul," might be reworded to "Confession is good for your marriage as well." Plus – maybe you will get some more cookies.

Day 55

SEX, SEX, SEX!

Scripture – "Husbands, in the same way be considerate as you live with your wives, and treat them with respect as the weaker partner and as heirs with you of the gracious gift of life, so that nothing will hinder your prayers. Finally, all of you, be like-minded, be sympathetic, love one another, be compassionate and humble." I Peter 3:7-8

Ok – now that I have your attention, let me acknowledge that when many of you see or hear the topic of sex broached in a discussion, a plethora of feelings may wash over you. For some it may involve thoughts of connection and intimacy – for others, an ongoing battleground. While I doubt that tips here are going to radically change your sexual landscape, it is my desire to at least generate some new thinking on the subject. So – here we go.

Today's tip is primarily for guys, but most women will probably nod their heads in agreement. A study that came out of the Gottman Institute in Seattle, reported that there is a direct correlation between sexual engagement and the willingness of partners to share in the day to day running of their lives. Specifically, men who do housework have more sex than men who don't. Women, in this study, found their husbands who contributed to housework and childcare as having greater sex appeal than couples in which the husband was chore-free.

Now guys, don't get confused and just think it is a simple cause and effect scenario – "do the laundry = sex," "load the dishwasher = sex." What the study revealed was that sexiness is directly connected to partnering – sharing the day to day events, details, and struggles of life. "Wait – are you saying that I should be actually living life with my mate as genuine partners?" Yes! "And when I do, by virtue of a deeper level of connectedness, I will be desired at a more intimate level?" Yes!

I know, it is easy to think – "Well, duh," but many have little or no sexual connection with their mate because they are not engaged in a true joint venture in life.

Purposeful Action: If you want to improve your intimacy – begin by getting in the trenches with your spouse and doing life together. Specifically, be aware of the domestic needs of your household. While I recognize that various occupational arrangements or demands may impact how you as a couple determine household responsibilities, I also know that the ways in which you view these issues works best when it is a shared, teamed, partnered approach. Commit to being a fully engaged companion.

Day 56

Bring Back Fun

Scripture –"There is a time for everything, and a season for every activity under heaven. . . a time to weep and a time to laugh, a time to mourn and a time to dance . . ." Ecclesiastes 3:1 & 4

Remember when you used to look forward to getting home to your spouse, when you couldn't wait to have the weekend together? Remember when the relationship was fun? For some, fun was two kids and twenty years ago. But for most, fun was a central part of your relationship early on. In a university study a few years ago, over 300 couples were studied to find the essential ingredients to long-term, happy, healthy marriages. One of those key elements was fun – including humor and playfulness. Many marriages today suffer from dry rot and have become what one wife summed up as: "Dull, dull, dull." While we may readily acknowledge that our relationships have defaulted to this hum drum place, we wonder just how we go about changing it. Let me suggest some possible steps.

- First, we need to **Be Playful.** Remember how you used to call each other pet names? Playful intimacy like that is important and can transcend the years of marriage.
- Secondly, **Surprise Each Other.** This can range from doing an unexpected deed for her to buying

a candy bar for him. It doesn't have to be expensive and it lets the other person know that you were thinking about them while you were apart.

- Thirdly, **Relax.** By this I mean, let your guard down. Marriage doesn't have to always be so serious. You don't need to feel guilty leaving your children to carve out a special evening with your mate. You may be parents, respected in your profession, and valued in your Church – but it is still ok to be silly and have a good time with your husband or wife.

So, there you are – you now officially have permission to be goofy with your spouse – and enjoy it.

Purposeful Action: Be playful, surprise each other, relax – put at least one of these into play today. I recognize that life gets intense and it may have been awhile since any of these have been on your radar. But take a risk. Be creative. Maybe even be ridiculous. But very simply, do something! Do something today to bring back some fun into your relationship.

 *Day 57*

"I Have the Power!"

Scripture – "The tongue has the power of life and death." Proverbs 18:21a

When my boys were young, they used to watch the cartoon series "He Man." From those decades ago, the theme song still echoes in my head along with the picture of "He Man" standing with his sword stretched out above his head, proclaiming those words, "I have the power."

While I may not have the kind of super-hero power that he possessed, I do have immense power to affect my spouse's self-concepts. And now that I think about it, I may feel that I need some of those super-hero strengths because I am often times competing with a warped culture that holds its own powers of influence.

I am speaking today particularly about body image. You cannot turn on the T.V. or sit through a movie without hearing a very strong message. One that screams out - "Unless you look like (plug in some actor or super model's name here), you are not good enough. And if you are not good enough, rest assured, your spouse will find someone better." She may be someone half your age whose body hasn't begun to sag yet or he may be the guy with the six-pack abs that look like they were purchased at the nearest fitness center.

And it isn't just the media that creates this insecurity. When we drool at the image on the screen or our eyes follow the body walking down the street, we create it too. We contribute to our spouse's not feeling "good enough" and their fears that we are on the hunt to find the "perfect body" that they are convinced that they don't have.

We are in competition with a twisted, but powerful, culture in the battle for our partner's heart and the safe and secure haven that we want to create for them. I don't know about you, but I love my spouse as she is and desire for her to absolutely rest in that knowledge.

Purposeful Action: Consider your words, your non-verbal expressions, and how you communicate those things that matter to your spouse. Because, "You have the power." You have the power to influence your partner's self-image. Find a specific opportunity today to assure them that you have eyes only for them. Be concrete as you battle for their heart.

Day 58

Childolatry

Scripture – "For this reason a man will leave his father and mother and be united to his wife, and the two will become one flesh." "Each one of you also must love his wife as he loves himself, and the wife must respect her husband." Ephesians 5:31 & 33

I know that this isn't an actual word, but it is a term I came across recently that I thought was very fitting. Elevating our children to a level of priority that was never intended and is actually unhealthy for all involved is to what "childolatry" refers.

Studies consistently report that couples who do more things together alone are happier. Yet, a large number of parents today are spending increased time parenting their children and less time with each other – doing things together such as entertaining friends or engaging in leisure activities. As one author expressed it, "We expect more from our marriages but feed them less." "The end of the 'go out and play, and don't come home till dinner' era has sucked the life out of our marriages."

Paralleling this trend are the findings that in the past 20 years we have seen a generation of children who have had to do little on their own, are more financially dependent on their parents, and are moving back home in increasing numbers.

How did this happen? The answers range from, "We want to make life easier for our kids," to "Their other parent and I went through a divorce over which I feel guilt. Requiring less of them makes me feel better." The bottom line is – we did it.

Whatever the reason for this change in focus, if we want our relationship with our spouse to be strong and healthy, we have to make that focus the number one priority. Together we will parent our kids. But before long, they will be off beginning their own journey. Who will be left then? Don't wait until then to discover that you are living with a stranger. Decide today to schedule time to connect with your spouse. As author John Gartner so aptly expressed, "On airplanes, in the event of an emergency, we are instructed to put the oxygen mask on our own faces first, and then on the children. Perhaps we need to do the same with our marriages."

Purposeful Action: It is easy to be guilty of having elevated our kids to an unrightful place of priority over our spouse. If this describes you, perhaps the first needed step today is to confess this mistake to your spouse and ask their forgiveness. Secondly, I want to urge you to communicate that you are putting them back in the role of #1 in your life. You might do this in a conversation but it is even more convincing if you do with your time. Carve out an evening, a date, or even a weekend get-a-way for just the two of you. It may require some planning, but it can effectively communicate what is really important in a relationship.

Day 59

The 3 Minute Argument

Scripture – "A gentle answer turns away wrath, but a harsh word stirs up anger." Proverbs 15:1

As I sat in my office yesterday, a couple recounted an argument that they had on Valentine's Day (Not the best day to argue). In actuality, they were both attempting to make the day romantic and special, but somehow managed to miscommunicate something that should have been minor and easily cleared up. But it wasn't.

First, one expressed some hurt over not feeling important. Then the other expressed defensiveness. From there, voices were raised and hurtful words were spoken. One retreated to the bedroom. In a few minutes, the other one followed, speaking more harsh words. After that person left the room, then the other one followed spewing equal amounts of venom. Needless to say, nothing was solved. What should have been a romantic evening spiraled into an emotional heap, and here they were in my office feeling both discouraged and unloved.

Relational expert John Gottman, of the University of Washington, has discovered that the most important points in an argument can be found in the first three minutes. What typically follows that, is the individuals just repeating the same points but at increased decibels. For me the take-aways from his research are this: 1) make your points (which will only take three minutes), and then 2) listen for understanding.

When my highest goal in a discussion is more about my desire to understand than it is my desire to force the other person to understand my point of view, there is greater likelihood of peaceful resolution.

Purposeful Action: In your next serious discussion – this could be a challenging topic, a disagreement, hurt feelings, and so on - observe the 3 minute rule. Agree to make your point and then listen, with the emphasis on understanding. I promise you that if you will both work towards understanding the other's point of view, genuinely trying to see what they see and why they see it that way, three minute discussions instead of three hour arguments can become the norm. And your relationship will benefit.

Day 60

What are the Warning Signs?

Scripture – "Can a man scoop fire into his lap without his clothes being burned? Can a man walk on hot coals without his feet being scorched?" Now then . . . listen to me; pay attention to what I say."
Proverbs 6:27-28 and 7:24

A couple of years ago, my wife and I were able to spend a few days in the Grand Canyon area. If you have never been there, you might think it is just a hole in the ground, which it is. But it is so much more. It is an incredible, beautiful, miraculous site that will take your breath away. You have to be there to really experience it.

But as gorgeous as the canyon is, it is also quite dangerous. As if you need to be reminded that a 5,000 foot drop could be deadly, there are warning signs everywhere about staying away from the edge. In spite of the cautions, people die there every year. In 2012 a young woman thought it would be great fun to have her picture taken next to a "Stay Away" sign so she could post it on Facebook. Yet as she climbed to get to the sign, rocks gave way and she fell to her death.

Too many times we similarly ignore the relational warnings; as you verbally bully your spouse to get your own way, he or she continues to distance themselves from you – until one day they are gone; flirting with your co-worker was exciting and didn't seem too troublesome, until it became a full blown affair and cost you your job and your reputation; you knew that making that connection on Facebook with the old sweetheart was not smart but you enjoyed the attention – until it cost you your marriage.

We have all seen those warning signs that indicate "Danger – Keep Back – this could cost you everything" but you have ventured onto the loose rock, thinking "I won't get caught – it can't happen to me." But when it does happen to you, you find that you would give anything to be able to go back and undo the damage. Now is your chance, before the edge gives way.

Purposeful Action: What are the relational warning signs that you know you should heed in your life? Perhaps it is the disrespectful tone you use to communicate frustration with your mate. Or maybe you are getting too close to a risky relational edge. Identify one warning sign that you need to pay closer attention to in order to preserve the health of your marriage. I encourage you to examine it closely, then turn and get safely back behind the perimeter. Embrace your partner tightly – and don't let go!

 *Day 61*

A Hug a Day Keeps the Doctor Away

Scripture – "Dear friends, let us love one another, for love comes from God. Everyone who loves has been born of God and knows God." I John 4:7

Do you like hugs? Now that may seem like a silly question. I mean, come on – remember when you first went out with that special someone. You were intrigued by their wit. You were dazzled by the sparkle in their eyes. And when the moment came that he or she hugged you, you felt – tingles, warmth, special, cared for – something. It felt good and you most likely looked forward to more hugs.

But for many who have been married for a few years, hugs may not come with the same frequency that they once did. What happened? Busy schedules, different priorities, or perhaps relational strife?

A recent study out of Carnegie Mellon University examined the science of hugs (I'll bet you never thought of hugs in terms of science before). What they discovered shouldn't be too surprising. Hugs were associated with lower blood pressure and reduced levels of the stress hormone cortisol. People who experienced frequent hugs seemed to be protected from a higher risk of getting sick when under stress.

So, what is the correlation of all of this for you? Simply put – give and receive more hugs from your partner and you may experience less sickness and stress. Now I am well aware that if you are at odds or in conflict with your spouse this may be difficult and will require other work on your relationship. But for many, the lack of hugs aren't necessarily as a result of conflict as much as they are just having forgotten how important they are and how much you enjoy them.

Purposeful Action: While I recognize that today's action may be more difficult than it sounds, it is important for your health, as well as that of your husband or wife, as well as the health of the relationship – hug your spouse, then repeat, repeat, repeat . . . . . but don't stop with just today. Endeavor to make this a lifelong pattern.

Day 62

Delay!

Scripture – "Therefore, as God's chosen people, holy and dearly loved, clothe yourselves with compassion, kindness, humility, gentleness and patience."
Colossians 3:12

As I recently sat listening to a couple, I was aware of just how quickly they were headed towards divorce. This is in part because they want all of their problems and conflicts solved immediately – if not sooner. And because of their impatience, they were barreling towards the divorce cliff. Yet – this doesn't have to happen. We live in a culture that says every issue must be solved immediately or else I need to take drastic action today. But my advice is – delay.

There was a study conducted a number of years ago that examined unhappy couples. The research team studied 5,232 married adults. Of these individuals, 645 reported being unhappily married. Five years later, these same adults were interviewed again. Some had divorced or separated and some had remained married. The results of the interviews were astounding. Among those who initially rated their marriages as "very unhappy" but remained together, nearly 80 percent considered themselves "happily married" and "much happier" five years later. Surprisingly, the opposite was found to be true for those who divorced. Of all the unhappy spouses in the initial survey, only 19 percent of those who got divorced or separated were happy five years later.

What does this say to us? Delay, delay delay! And not just divorce but any destructive behavior. Your partner has been inconsiderate or unkind today and you want to zing him back immediately. Delay. Your spouse has withheld affection or communication and you want to show her how it feels. Delay. Your husband or wife has hurt your deeply for the last time and you want out. Delay.

Purposeful Action: There is always time to take rash action, and sometimes there is even the need to, but don't be in a hurry to get there. Delay – because there is no substitute for time. Because of God's grace, He is patient and often delays in how He deals with us – giving us the time we need to make better choices. Today, whether you experience a conflict, disagreement, or some other issue that screams "I need resolution," I encourage you to delay, give space and time that allows for contemplation as well as communicates respect to the other person. If you don't resolve it today, there is always tomorrow. And it is just possible that you both may have gained a clearer perspective in the light of a new day.

 *Day 63*

Did Your Partner Change on You?

Scripture – "When I was a child, I talked like a child,
I thought like a child, I reasoned like a child. When I
became a man, I put childish ways behind me. Now
we see but a poor reflection as in a mirror, then we
shall see face to face." I Corinthians 13:11-12a

I sometimes hear couples complain about one another, saying things such as "You are not the person that I married." At first glance, we may think, "Yea, I hate it when you marry someone and then they change on you." We feel cheated or that this was a bait and switch. You fell in love with one person but when you got them home, you discovered that they were really somebody else.

While this can happen, I want to ask you to consider another thought. Is it possible that they were not deceiving you, but that they really did change? When you think about it, are you the same person that you were five years ago? Probably not. You see, we all are constantly changing. Unless we are a hermit living in a cave on a remote island, we are growing and changing because we interact with different people and we continually learn new information.

But the fact that we all change – both you and your mate, doesn't need to be a negative. I realize that individuals often fear change in their mate because they are afraid that he or she will outgrow them and won't need them anymore. Yet it can be exciting to rediscover our partner as he or she continues to develop. Actually, if we are open to growth in both ourselves and our spouse, acceptance of this single concept of inevitable change might contribute to keeping our relationship from getting boring and stale.

Purposeful Action: My suggestion for you today is simply to look for one thing in your significant other that has changed from when you first met him or her that has been a positive. Then tell them how much you appreciate that characteristic or quality. Embracing change could be the beginning of falling in love all over again. And that's pretty exciting.

Day 64

The Importance of Remembering

Scripture – "Each of you is to take up a stone on his shoulder . . . to serve as a sign among you. In the future, when your children ask you, "What do these stones mean?" tell them . . ." Joshua 4:5b-6

Recorded in the book of Joshua, chapters 3 and 4, is the account of Israel crossing the Jordan River during the season when the river was at flood stage. It is an amazing story of the power of God to do miraculous things. One of the interesting pieces to the story is that God instructed the Israelites to select 12 men to each carry a stone on his shoulder out of the Jordan. These stones were then set up in plain view to serve as a reminder to the people of what God had orchestrated for the nation on that day.

Remembering – an important concept that we sometimes overlook. Historically we have made it a point as a country to designate national holidays around events, such as: the Fourth of July, Memorial Day, Thanksgiving, and so on. These are for the purpose of remembering – but are often simply used as a time for barbeques and family get togethers. While there is nothing wrong with these gatherings, we have often lost sight of the significance of remembering these special days.

Similarly, in relationships, we often take significant events for granted, such as – when we first began to date our spouse, wedding anniversaries, and other memorable events. We make jokes about how husbands fail to remember anniversaries and birthdays because many times we have lost the art of remembering. But it is not just remembering – it is acknowledging the importance of the event, celebrating the event, relishing the event and the person who gives it significance.

God gave Joshua instructions about the stones because He knows how prone we are to forget things that are important. And when we forget, we make everything common. What do you need to recall today about your relationship with your spouse? You married that person because they were anything but common – they stood out from all the rest. They were special!

Purposeful Action: Think back through the significant milestones of your martial relationship, looking particularly at some of the "firsts" – first date, first holiday together, the day you became engaged – you get the idea. Now select one that you can call attention to in an especially honoring way. It may involve watching a wedding video, going to the restaurant where you first went to dinner, and so on. By finding new and creative ways to acknowledge these events in your life, you are reinforcing the significance of your life-long journey together.

Day 65

What are You Feeding?

Scripture – "He who guards his lips guard his life, but he who speaks rashly will come to ruin."
Proverbs 13:3

You come in from work exhausted to the smell of freshly baked bread. Following the scent, you head for the kitchen but along with way you trip over a toy carelessly left in your path. Immediately your blood begins to boil. Arriving in the kitchen you find your spouse who is baking the bread along with the culprit (your child) who left the toy laying around. What are the first words that will most likely come out of your mouth?

There is a Native American story in which an elderly Cherokee is teaching his grandson about life. The grandfather explains that there is a terrible fight going on inside of him. The fight is between two wolves – one urging him toward peace, love, self-confidence, and compassion. The other drives him toward revenge, regret, self-pity, and resentment. The grandson asked, "Which wolf will win?" The grandfather replied, "The one I feed."

We have all probably found ourselves in a situation similar to the one above, as the spouse coming in from work. Irritants abound, to which we can easily and harshly respond. And yet, if we can catch ourselves and hit the "pause" button before we respond, we just might be able to modify our reaction before we negatively impact those whom we love.

We all have the capacity to love with our words and actions or to damage and destroy another with the same. So the question with which you are faced is a simple one – which one will you feed?

Purposeful Action: The next time you find yourself, annoyed, irritated, or fuming mad – allow those feelings to act as a warning gauge, as though they were a question. "Which one will you feed?" Catch yourself before you stumble into words that you will wish you could take back. Instead choose – actively choose to feed love and compassion.

Day 66

Text Your Way to Intimacy?

Scripture – "And let us consider how we may spur one another on toward love and good deeds."
Hebrew 10:24

Texting and smart phones have brought the world to our fingertips in so many ways. While our parents didn't have access to these tools growing up, we do. They are now a source of both enhanced communication as well as never ending distraction.

One research study discovered that nearly 20% of couples feel closer to each other as a result of exchanging messages through texting. I can fully relate to this as my wife and I send each other brief messages through the workday, which lets us each know that the other is thinking about us.

However, as a couple shared with me this week, trying to text about major conflicts and issues more often results in poor communications, misunderstandings, and flared tempers. When we attempt to have major exchanges through texting, we miss body language and other non-verbal cues as well as tone of voice. These are critical to increased understanding.

The study went on to point out that the amount of time spent online and texting has been a source of distraction for many couples. Twenty-five percent of cell-phone owners surveyed indicated that they felt unimportant when their partner was focused on his or her cell phone when they were together. This has been the source of arguments which can have a distancing effect on many couples.

Purposeful Action: So, three suggestions: 1) If you need to talk with your partner about something significant – do it in person; 2) give people you are with priority over your cellphone – the virtual world will be there later, so put the phone away; and 3) be intentional today about reaching out to your mate, using texting in ways that will let him or her know how much they matter.

Day 67

What Do You See?

Scripture – "We demolish arguments and every pretension that sets itself up against the knowledge of God, and we take captive every thought to make it obedient to Christ." 2 Corinthians 10:5

Duringa recent dinner conversation, while enjoying some great Mexican food, my friend Ed, who refurbishes houses, began to talk about different kinds of wall texturing. In his house they have a hand troweled texture as opposed to the sprayed type. During the discussion, he mentioned that in one room of their house they sometimes pick out faces on the wall. They will ask each other in the family, "So, what face did you see on that wall today?"

As our conversation about this continued (no doubt, a result of too much chips and salsa), Ed pointed out that they don't always see the same thing. One day they might pick out a kind face in the texture while the next day what they notice is perhaps more sinister. He has observed that different family members, as well as guests, see different things, and they find that what they see is even affected by the mood they are in on a given day.

Ok – weird thoughts today, you may be thinking. But as we talked about wall texture and faces, I couldn't help but think about how we react to each other based upon what we think we see. Our spouse, child, or co-worker say something to us today and we take it in stride. But tomorrow they may make the same statement and we are hurt or offended. And even still, on a different day, we may find their words intriguing or even humorous. What's the deal?

Communication can be so very fragile. How we hear and see things is affected by our mood and what is going on in our life. Typically we begin listening with a set of assumptions – good or bad, which then colors how we hear and receive things.

Purposeful Action: Today I want you to try something – begin every conversation with your partner, as you are listening, with a positive set of assumptions. This is part of a process of "taking every thought captive." Assume that he or she cares about you and is not out "to get you." While they may or may not have your best interests at heart, beginning with optimistic assumptions will dramatically affect how you hear and receive their communication which could easily escalate into healthy dynamics. Give it a try. Who knows, you might see something on that relational wall that you've never seen before. And it just might be wonderful!

Day 68

Why?

Scripture – "Set a guard over my mouth, O Lord;
keep watch over the door of my lips." Psalm 141:3

"Why did you let the kids run around in the backyard in their pajamas?" "Why did you eat donuts for dinner?" "Why didn't you do your homework?" "Why did you say such a hurtful thing?" We ask "why" a lot. We ask it of our kids, our spouse, and sometimes those whom we supervise at work. Why do we ask why?

Now you are probably thinking – well, I ask why because I want to know. Perhaps. But there are many occasions when we ask "why," not because we want an answer, but because we are upset. Think about it. What is the correct answer to "Why did you eat donuts for dinner?" If the answer is, "Because they sounded good," will you be satisfied? Will that make it ok? How about, "Why didn't you do your homework?" If your child responds with, "Because I didn't want to," are you libel to respond with, "Well, that's ok then. Thanks for telling me?"

We frequently ask "why" questions when actually a more appropriate response would be – "I feel unloved when you say such hurtful things." But instead of responding in an emotionally honest manner, we ask "why." If you are on the receiving end of the question, "why" can feel very accusatory. Which may be what you want the person to feel. But you have put them in a position to be wrong no matter what they answer. When we ask "Why did you let the kids run around in the backyard in their pajamas?" there is a hidden statement that the other person may hear as "You are an unworthy parent and should not be trusted with the children." When we feel accused, we typically either respond defensively or we withdraw and shut down.

Purposeful Action: When you find yourself about to ask "why," first, pause and examine whether this is truly an answerable question. Second, while you may feel a bit more vulnerable, see if instead of asking a question you can make a clear and honest statement. Making more feeling statements as opposed to asking "why" will often give individuals a sense value, which they will appreciate.

Day 69

Is it Worth Clutching?

Scripture – "It is a man's honor to avoid strife, but every fool is quick to quarrel." Proverbs 20:3

There is a tribe in South America that has discovered a creative way to catch monkeys. Taking a large gourd with a long narrow neck, they put fruit inside it and place it in an area frequented by monkeys. When a monkey smells the fruit, they instinctively go the gourd, look inside and, seeing the prize, reach in to the bottom and grab the fruit. Though he attempts to pull the fruit out, he is unsuccessful. You see his hand was open when he reached in but once he has grabbed the fruit his hand will no longer fit through the opening. Now you and I can survey the situation and clearly know what needs to be done – let go of the fruit.

Unfortunately, those monkeys don't think to let go. Instead they struggle and struggle to get their hand out. But as long as their grasp is tight, they are stuck. They want what they want and their unrelenting grasp will lead to certain death. Oh what foolish creatures.

But I wonder, are we really that different? We sometimes find ourselves engaged in a conflict or argument with our spouse. It is truly a meaningless argument, and we know it. But now that we are engaged, we want to win – sometimes, at all costs. We may say mean and hurtful things, we may attempt to manipulate things to our advantage. We can see that our mate is getting more hurt by the minute. We know we should stop talking before it is too late. But instead, we continue to clutch our need to be right and to win. I have seen far too many couples teeter on the brink of marital death all because they won't release their grasp.

Purposeful Action: Don't die on one of those meaningless hills that will only serve to alienate your spouse. Strive to recognize when you are engrossed in a battle that has become about "winning" rather than "resolving." Because truly, when you "win" one of these encounters – you and your spouse both lose and your marriage is dealt another needless blow. Let go of your "grasp" to win with a more powerful motivation of a desire to love.

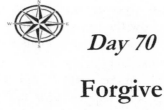

Day 70

Forgive

Scripture – "For if you forgive men when they sin against you, your heavenly Father will also forgive you." Matthew 6:14

"Violation" is not a word that we use frequently (unless we spend lots of time in traffic court for speeding), but it is one that we often feel. Someone ignores or disrespects us, they take something of ours that doesn't belong to them, they disregard our feelings, and the list goes on and on. When these things happen, we feel violated and we may even try to dish out "pay back." Yet when we do this, rarely do we feel good about it.

You see, we serve an Almighty God, who is all about forgiveness. Scriptures indicate that His forgiveness of our sins is frequently connected to our willingness to forgive others who have wronged us. While it may be an easy concept for us to intellectually grasp – it can be tough as nails to follow through on with those we love – especially if they have gravely wronged us in some manner. Yet, research indicates that those couples who both seek forgiveness from each other as well as offer it, are more successful in their relationships. I want to offer four steps that you may find helpful in forgiving your mate.

1) Try to take a break from focusing on what happened and how the person wronged you. It is too easy to get caught up in a singular focus that blocks out all rational thinking.

2) Be intentional about NOT punishing the individual. This can happen with unkind harsh words, pouting, belittling, and continual reminders of their mistakes.

3) Give your memory a break. Actively work to "let go" of thoughts about what transpired.

4) Actively redirect your thinking. Give up your "right" to respond in kind. It is easy to hold on to resentment and hang on to your desire to retaliate. Make a conscious decision instead to work for the other person's good.

Holding tightly to your anger and unwillingness to forgive can sometimes feel good, in the short run. But in the end it can turn sour and toxic in your soul.

Purposeful Action: Identify one resentment you have been emotionally hanging onto regarding a perceived violation by your spouse. Write it on a piece of paper, with details about the wrong and your associated feelings. Ask God to help you to let go of this hurt, tear up the paper and resolve in your heart to be truly done with this issue. Finally, there is no need to ever tell your husband or wife what you just did, because you are not going for brownie points but for forgiveness.

Day 71

How Do You Want to Be Remembered?

Scripture –"A happy heart makes the face cheerful, but heartache crushes the spirit." Proverbs 15:13

This is a question that many of us ponder, particularly as we get older. Sometimes the answer I hear from an employee might be, "I want to be remembered as a hard and productive worker;" from a neighbor, "as a loyal and trusted friend;" or from a parent, "that I was always there for my kids." But I wonder how you would like your spouse to remember you?

Hmm – as you ponder that you are probably hoping that he or she will have fond memories of perhaps love, faithfulness and companionship. And yet, I see far too many who, unfortunately, may only remember their partner as an unhappy, domineering curmudgeon.

Comedian Carol Burnette was recently asked in an interview how she wants to be remembered. She replied, "That I made somebody laugh when they needed it, That at one point, when they needed it, that I made them forget – even if it is just for 10 seconds – that they were hurting."

Now I am certainly not suggesting that you can tell a joke and erase the world's problems. I also am not proposing that getting your spouse to laugh will resolve all of your marital conflicts. However, what I would urge you to consider is this – it is likely that your spouse married you, in part, because you had a good time together, enjoyed each other's company, and probably shared a few (maybe lots) laughs together. But I wonder – would they say that those things are still true, or has the seriousness of life's hurts and difficulties put a permanent scowl on your face.

The bottom line today – life is easier when we can lighten the mood of everyday challenges with a regular dose of humor.

Purposeful Action: Make it your goal to bring a smile to your partner's face today. You might accomplish this with a little silliness, sharing a funny story, or, if you are like me, being able to laugh at your own goofy blunders, like running into the same tree limb for the fifth time. By the way, did you hear the one about the Big Brown Burly Bulgarian Bear who walked into . . . . . ."

Day 72

Sex

Scripture – "Do to others as you would have them do to you." Luke 6:31

On a previous day we looked at the Gottman Institute study that demonstrated a connection between day to day partnering and increased levels of sexual intimacy. Over time, the study determined, that the sexual connection was sustained when the wife felt respected and understood. And these two components are communicated by accepting influence from one another and being responsive to each other's feelings.

So often, it is this lack of being sensitive to the needs of the other that results in stonewalling and defensiveness. Invariably there are times, when for any number of reasons, a spouse may say "no" to a partner's sexual advances. What happens next is critical to a couple's long-term emotional and sexual health.

If a partner communicates annoyance or responds curtly with a disgusted "Fine!" there is a cost in this form of punishment. The rejected pursuer may say indignantly, "I don't really want to have sex with you anyway!" This leads to a rejection of the other person, and over time, this mutually punishing interaction leads to a level of toxicity that can kill a marriage.

A number of years ago, a couple came into my office whose experiences, like that above, led to a five year stalemate as they each waited for the other to come out of their respective corner to make the first sexual move. They both were wounded, feeling punished, rejected, and undesirable. Unfortunately, they had managed to drain all remaining life out of their marriage before they ever got to my office.

A much healthier response to a "No," would be something like, "I really appreciate your telling me that you are exhausted from the day. I understand and respect that. So, what would you like to do?" If you can unselfishly respond to the "no" positively, you will communicate the very understanding that sustains long-term sexual health.

Purposeful Action: Sexual intimacy can be a tricky topic for lots of couples. Make it your goal to communicate in your words and behavior – respect and understanding of his or her feelings at every opportunity. Yes, I know this can be difficult if there has been a lack of intimacy for a while. But truly demonstrating sensitivity to the each other is one of the pillars that is foundational to genuine connection. Sex is an event while intimacy is the environment of the relationship. Take one intentional step today toward creating a safe and welcoming environment for your partner.

Day 73

Still Dating?

Scripture – "A new command I give you: Love one another. As I have loved you, so you must love one another." John 13:34

I remember a story from a number of years ago, that a friend related regarding his parents. He said that when he was growing up, his "normal" was different from that of many of his school friends. He related that his parents kissed in the kitchen every morning, his dad brought his mom flowers once a week, and that his parents went out on a "date" at least twice a week. They even got away a few times a year for romantic weekends. He didn't think much of his parent's "normal" until he encountered friends who experienced a very different reality. Many of them had parents who fought frequently, rarely had a civil conversation, and almost never went out on dates. And of course, there were numerous friends whose parent's marriages had deteriorated into divorce.

Likewise, I remember my friend who lived across the street from me when I was in Jr. High school, whose parents would sit in the living room for the first half hour when his dad arrived home from work. The children, actually no one, was allowed to infringe upon that time. It was a sacred time for the couple to debrief after the day of work; to catch-up; and most of all, to reconnect.

Frequently, newlyweds start making their relationship a priority in similar ways. But then after a few years of marriage, socializing with friends, children coming on to the scene, and any number of other intrusions become priority – and complacency creeps into the relationship. If not caught, it can take over and even erode the underpinnings of the marriage.

What did the two couples described above know that many seem to miss? Something relatively simple but profound. If I water my garden (continue to nurture my marriage), it will grow. If I fail to tend to it, it will die.

Purposeful Action: I encourage you to closely examine the health of your marriage today. See what has suffered due to busy schedules and complacency. Now, recall one of the ways you used to make it a priority. Right now – turn to your spouse if you are with them, and if not, call or text them and say to them your own paraphrase of something along the lines of, "I used to get excited and look forward to our dates together. I treasured those times because I love you. However, I know that life has become busy and sometimes complicated – perhaps even problematic. I know that I have probably not made you the priority that I once did and that is not acceptable. I want to change that. So, would you do me the honor of going with me this Saturday to _____ (fill in the blank)?" Modify as needed.

Day 74

Black Friday

Scripture – "You have stolen my heart . . . my bride; you have stolen my heart with one glance of your eyes. . ." Song of Solomon 4:9

Ok – before you start to think that this is another "Black Friday" ad, I promise – it is not. You have no doubt had your fill of those over the years. We were sitting on Thanksgiving afternoon a couple of years ago watching ad after ad each declaring the unbelievable deals that their particular store would have on "Black Friday" – beginning at 6:00 pm on Thursday. When? My wife chuckled as I kept telling the TV that "Friday is not Thursday."

On Friday my son posted the following:
"Black Friday Through the Years"
2005: 5 AM
2010: 3 AM
2012: 12 AM
2013 Thursday 8 PM
2014: Thursday
2020: 4th of July

Now that may be an exaggerated prediction – or perhaps not. Time will tell. The morning after Thanksgiving (sometimes referred to as Friday), my wife's phone blew up with 36 "Black Friday" emails. While I find the greed of "Black Friday" overwhelming, that is a discussion for another time. What I want to observe for today are the extremes that the marketplace will go to in order to capture your business. They will start sales earlier and earlier; their advertising creativity will continue to entice; and efforts to outdo each other to snag your money will seem endless.

But as much as I may dislike the commercialism of it all, I can learn from their determination to not give up until that have my last dollar. What if we went to the same effort to convince our mate of our love? I could give her a present for our anniversary. Or, perhaps, our anniversary could start the day before. Maybe we could give a sneak preview a week earlier. Ok – I may be getting carried away. But my point is simply this – if we used the strategies of "Black Friday" merchants to convince our spouses of our love – he or she would have NO trouble knowing it.

Purposeful Action: So the question for you is – do you love your mate as much as Walmart or Best Buy love your money? If so, then spend a few minutes today contemplating how to convince him or her with your own advertising campaign. Perhaps you need to print up your own "ad" on the computer or a coupon promising some free offer when they come home from work. You might even create a humorous video on your phone and send it to your spouse inviting them to your special occasion sale. Have some fun with us.

Day 75

That's Not Marriage

Scripture – "Trust in the Lord with all your heart and lean not on your own understanding; in all your ways submit to Him, and He will make your paths straight." Proverbs 3:5-6

A few months ago I heard a speaker talk about his years of pastoring a church in Arkansas. During his time there, he had a gentleman in the church who was a Fish and Games Official. This came in pretty handy as this official would periodically call him to tell him where they had recently stocked with fish. He might say, "Well we just put 1000 trout in a particular stream," or "We dumped a load of 500 Catfish in such and such a lake."

The pastor would then take his kids to one of these locations to fish. They had such a great time as they would cast their line in – and pull out a fish. Cast it in again – and pull out anther fish. The kids loved it.

Once, when the family went camping, they discovered a nearby lake. So, the dad asked his children if they wanted to go fishing. With an excited "yes," off they went. His daughter cast in her line – then pulled it out. She cast it in again, but still nothing. She looked at her dad and said, "Something is wrong." The father told her that sometimes you have to be patient and wait for the fish to bite. Disappointed, she proclaimed, "This isn't fishing." To which her dad said, "Actually, this is. What you have done before really isn't."

How often have we watched the couple on the movie screen run in slow motion, embracing one another, completely fulfilling each other's deepest desires every moment of their day? Yet when we go home – we do so to noisy children, a broken water heater, and an angry spouse. We may then find ourselves thinking, "This isn't marriage." Well, actually it is. What we saw on the cinema screen is not an accurate portrayal.

Having realistic expectations, when it comes to the ups and downs of our marital life, is essential. It enables us to better accept and appreciate our mate and the dynamics of our relationship.

Purposeful Action: It might be educational (and maybe even entertaining) to watch a romantic comedy with your husband or wife, agreeing to take notes together of everything that takes place in the movie that is a bit outlandish or at least somewhat over the top. Then once the movie is over, have a conversation regarding the deeper connections as well as the messiness of an authentic relationship. Embrace the reality of loving a flawed individual – who is also doing the same. Let the adventure begin.

Day 76

Words Generate Feelings

Scripture – "Therefore encourage one another and build each other up." I Thessalonians 5:11

As Jennie sat with her friend Lisa over coffee, she said, "David is such a pig. He never cleans up his messes, he doesn't put anything away, he gets the milk out and then leaves it on the counter – his inconsideration is driving me crazy." Needless to say, Jennie was frustrated and felt safe expressing this to her friend.

However, the ongoing sequence led to wounded feelings. You see her friend Lisa shared this conversation with her husband Tony and in turn Tony relayed it back to David. As you can imagine, David went home to Jennie, angry and hurt. Not an uncommon reaction.

While Jennie's complaint certainly had legitimacy, the problem that the above exchange created was relational insecurity for David. It wasn't that David intended to be a slob, he just wasn't aware of the problem or her frustrations. Instead of telling David directly what she needed, she had gone to someone outside of the marriage to voice her complaints. This calls attention to an important principle - don't say anything about your partner that you are not willing to say to them.

When we talk negatively about our spouse to someone else, it anchors those negative feelings without doing anything to resolve the situation. Each of us wants to believe two things: 1) that our spouse is coming directly to us with problems and concerns and 2) that he or she is building us up to the outside world. We never want to feel that our relationship is being undermined.

Purposeful Action: While most of us have slipped at one time or another in this area, I encourage you to make a conscious effort today to say what needs to be said, directly to your mate. Be specifically aware of how you speak about him or her to others. Make it your goal to paint your spouse in the best light possible to others, in the same way that you desire for them to speak to others about you; accentuate the positives. It will lead to different and more positive feelings about your husband or wife for you, and they in turn will also feel valued.

Day 77

Do You Know the Sound?

Scripture – "In this same way, husbands ought to love their wives as their own bodies. He who loves his wife loves himself. After all, no one ever hated their own body, but they feed and care for their body, just as Christ does the church." Ephesians 5:28-29

It is hard to believe that it has been 22 years since I built the house that we live in. Ok, I didn't exactly build it – the construction company did. However, while they were building it that spring and summer, the boys and I finished the basement while the builders were doing the main level.

Being intimately involved in the building process on a day to day basis allowed us to "know" the house well. As a result, I know when something sounds differently or out of whack. This was evident recently when my wife and I were sitting in the living room talking and one of the downstairs drain pumps came on. There are three different pumps in the mechanical room that serve different purposes. While my wife wasn't even aware that one had kicked on, I knew not only that one had engaged but I knew by the sound which one it was.

It made me wonder – do I know my wife as well as I know our house? Or for you, it might be – do you know your spouse as well as you know the sounds of the engine in your car or the sounds coming from your child's room? Are you intimately engaged with your spouse in such a manner that when he or she is unusually quiet, agitated, stressed, or hurt – that you would know? Or do you blow by them, oblivious to what is going on?

We all want to matter to our mate. We want to know that we are important to them – important enough that they notice what is going on within us. Do you know the sound of when things are out of sync?

Purposeful Action: Observe your spouse closely today, endeavoring to determine their emotional mindset. Watch facial expressions, listen to their tone of voice, notice their body language and see what you can learn. Now, based on what you noticed, respond to them with an appropriate expression of kindness and love.

Day 78

Are You Kidding Yourself?

Scripture – "Be completely humble and gentle; be patient, bearing with one another in love."
Ephesians 4:2

"Things will get better." This is a phrase of encouragement that we use with regularity. And it is often very true. For example, you are sad at the loss of a pet – "Things will get better." True. As we typically experience grief, experiences are integrated into our new normal and things do get better. We wake up today late, we realize the clothes we wanted to wear are dirty, and we are out of cereal for breakfast. We tell ourselves that things will get better, and they probably will.

But how about - you are gambling in Vegas, you are down $5,000 dollars. It was money you couldn't afford to lose and you sure can't afford to lose anymore. But you hit the ATM machine again, continuing to plop down your money on a particular number on the roulette wheel, saying, "Things will get better." Will they? Hmm – they might begin to get better if you keep your cash in your pocket, but probably not until then.

I regularly see couples distant from one another or embroiled in conflict state, "Oh well, things will get better." But then they don't. Why not? Because rarely do things really improve just by themselves. Things get better in my relationship when I – do things differently, learn to communicate more effectively, express kindness, speak words of love, honor my spouse's boundaries and requests, and a multitude of other decisions. Things get better when I take action. Otherwise, I am probably kidding myself.

Purposeful Action: As you think about the temperature of your significant relationship today, are there areas where things are not as you would like, that you simply address with "Things will get better?" Identify one issue in your relationship that you would like to see get better. Determine one step that you could take that might lead to improvement. Now – take that step. Do the very thing that you can do that could contribute to things getting better. Then, who knows – they just might.

Day 79

Unbelievable!

*Scripture – ". . . let us not love with words or speech
but with actions and in truth." I John 3:18*

Back during the Christmas holidays, I had the most unbelievable experience. My wife and I were out of town and had the opportunity to spend an afternoon and evening with a couple of my cousins and their spouses. We went to one of their homes, visited in the afternoon, went out to dinner, then came back and played a game until late in the evening.

Now you are thinking – ah, not too astounding so far – and you would be correct. Later as my wife and I were driving back to where we were staying and were reflecting on the fun of the evening, it dawned on me. During that entire time, probably seven hours, I never once saw anyone check their phone for messages or Facebook posts. Instead, everyone was engaging with each other. It almost felt as though we were experiencing some ancient tradition, some long lost art.

I have pretty much come to expect that separating individuals from their phones – whether eating, conversing, or doing pretty much anything, is the equivalent of asking them to not breathe or blink their eyes. It just can't be done. But I was reminded that it can be done – and it should be with much greater frequency.

Purposeful Action: How refreshing would it be to feel that you had your partner's undivided attention – to know that you weren't second to Mr. I-phone or Ms. Samsung Galaxy? So, try something new and create a phone-free time zone. It may be between dinner and bedtime - the phones are turned off or are in a different room. Or some other time – significant time, when your phones are not allowed to distract you from one another. Look into his or her eyes and engage in authentic undistracted conversation. My suspicion is that he or she will enjoy being #1 just as much as you do.

Day 80

Want to Suffer?

Scripture – "Also, if two lie down together, they will keep warm. But how can one keep warm alone?"
Ecclesiastes 4:11

As you read that title, you are probably thinking, "Of course not." And that echoes the sentiments of most of us. We hate suffering. We want comfort. We want to lay in a hammock, drink wine, nap, enjoy a massage – anything that pampers ourselves. But suffer – no thanks; I am happy to skip that.

In an interview last year, author Malcolm Gladwell was asked "What's the one thing you'd like us to take away from your book?" He responded with, "That the greatest things in the world come from suffering. It ought to give us solace. A lot of what is most beautiful about the world arises from struggle."

Before you conclude that he has lost his marbles, ponder that statement. Think about difficulties you and your significant other have struggled through. It might have been a complicated illness, financial issues, a sick child, or caring for parents. The list can go on and on. Yes, it is not unusual for some to allow these challenges to rip them apart. But for others, times of problem solving and getting in the trenches together can be what makes a team.

These events give us opportunity to learn to depend on each other. In doing so we learn that we are not alone in our troubles. Even in sports, when a team rises to the occasion to achieve victory, they often learn some things about themselves as well as their team, and they find that they have bonded in new and strengthening ways.

What struggles have you and your spouse experienced, that when you think back to those times, you discover feelings of satisfaction? In all likelihood they exist, you just have to stop and remember.

Purposeful Action: Sit down with your mate and remember – remember not just struggles but talk about the manner in which the two of you together overcame those challenges. Allow yourselves to experience that success and that wave of bonding all over again. Personally, I would say to my wife, "Do I want to suffer? Not really. But if I have to, I'd much rather do it with you."

Day 81

Intimacy – Where Did it Go?

Scripture – "I will search for the one my heart loves."
Song of Solomon 3:2b

Time and again I hear from couples who talk about their lost intimacy. It seemed to develop easily in the beginning of their marriage, but now . . . they are uncertain, intimidated, and even afraid of intimacy. But what happened?

King Solomon, in writing the book "Song of Songs" in the Bible, was composing a marriage love-making manual. In it he describes everything from the exclusivity of our marriage relationship – "My lover is mine and I am his" (2:16) to the powerful and protective nature of public display of affection – "He has taken me to the banquet hall, and his banner over me is love" (2:4). He goes into greater detail of lovemaking as well. But the powerful concept that I see communicated throughout this book is that making love with your spouse is a strong contributor to intimacy. And I am talking here about much more than just having sex.

Intimacy is developed over time and through a number of stages. This is one of the reasons that I commonly see couples who may have been married for years, and even had an active sex life, but have never really developed strong bonds of intimacy. But here is the cool thing – if you find yourself in that place, know that it is not too late to develop intimate connections with your spouse.

Purposeful Action: Today I want to suggest a few strategies that can be helpful in rekindling the passions that once existed.

- If lovemaking has gone stagnant, begin to reconnect with simple hand holding and gazing into each other's eyes. Your relationship probably originally began this way and it may be a stage you need to go through again. But I encourage you not to think of it as a stage just to get to somewhere else. It has ongoing merit all its own.

- For men – know that a woman's sexual desire is aroused when you meet her emotional needs and connect with her relationally. Take time to romance her outside of the bedroom.

- For women – remember that respect is a huge component for men and for a healthy relationship. Make sure that you communicate to him those areas where you respect him.

- Make it a priority to regularly express tenderness and affection with each other.

- Finally, strive to communicate your gratefulness for your partner, demonstrating the kind of love you had for him or her in the beginning of the relationship.

While these few steps are no guarantee that your sex life will be explosive, I would submit that they are critical pieces toward building healthier connections and in turn laying the foundation for greater intimacy.

Day 82

How are You at Serving?

Scripture – "When he had finished washing their feet, he put on his clothes and returned to his place. 'Do you understand what I have done for you?' he asked them. 'You call me 'Teacher' and 'Lord,' and rightly so, for that is what I am. Now that I, your Lord and Teacher, have washed your feet, you also should wash one another's feet." John 13:12-14

Who does the dishes in your house? It may be you, your spouse, the kids, or even the dog I suppose if you leave the dishes on floor. For lots of families this can be a point of contention. As kids I remember we would do anything we could to get out of doing the dishes. Usually one of us would have to wash and another one would have to dry. If you were the dryer, you would love it if you could find a speck of food left on a dish because then your sibling would have to re-wash it. Never mind that you would have to re-dry the dish. You were doing something you didn't like and if you could make more work for someone else, at least you felt like you had a little control. The furthest thing from your mind was serving.

Fast forward to adulthood. Now what does doing dishes look like? Well, one thing that is a little easier is that we have a dishwasher, but dishes still have to be loaded and unloaded. And, of course, now that you are an adult I'm sure you never still try to get out of doing the dishes do you?

With kids grown and gone, in our house it has become a different kind of game. When dinner is done, my wife and I will try to clear the table and load the dishes first because we truly try to out serve the other. My wife has even accused me of unloading the dishwasher when silverware and pans are nearly too hot to touch, just so I can beat her to it. Don't think I'm competitive or anything. Needless to say, neither one of us ever feel as though we are having to do more than our fair share of the work.

Purposeful Action: When we strive to out serve or out love our spouse, it always goes to a good place. Identify one area that neither you or your spouse get too excited about but explore ways that you can work to out serve him or her. Don't call attention to your effort, instead just, quietly, behind the scenes – serve.

Day 83

Be Vigilant

Scripture – "Be alert and of sober mind. Your enemy the devil prowls around like a roaring lion looking for someone to devour." I Peter 5:8

I want you to imagine that you just won the Publisher's Clearing House Sweepstakes. Ok – before you decide how to spend it all, keep imagining with me. So the Sweepstakes people show up to your house in an armored truck and deliver your winnings to you not in a check but in $100 bills. While you don't care what form they deliver it in, I mean money is money, but they deliver it to your front yard in dozens of boxes. Your challenge – people are standing around watching the delivery take place and your bank has promised to come and pick up the boxes for you but can't get there for three hours. What would you do?

If you are anything like me, you would probably stand guard over your money for the next three hours because the money is of great value to you. Makes sense. But how many have failed to vigilantly guard their marriage with the same watchful eye? You see, temptation surrounds us – those related to anger, sexual unfaithfulness, relational pressures, and many others. Do you tend to build a wall of protection around your marriage or do you treat it with a carelessness that communicates that it is not all that important to you? Do you value your relationship as much as the pile of money in the front yard?

Purposeful Action: While this may seem like a weird action, humor me and try it. I want you to calculate how much your spouse is worth. What? Yes, begin by figuring out how much it would cost to replace them – day care, house chores, changing diapers, carting the kids to piano lessons and hockey practices, as well as their income that they may bring to the table. Now add to that how much their personal support is worth – taking care of you when you have the flu, helping you shop for clothes or a computer, enduring holidays at the in-laws, and so on. I know this seems like an impossible feat, but try to calculate a monetary number. Now ask yourself the question – "How am I going to protect this 'sweepstake's winnings' until at the end of life, God returns to claim them?" Let the protection begin.

 *Day 84*

What I Learned in Kindergarten

Scripture – "By this everyone will know that you are my disciples, if you love one another." John 13:35

Today's children learn to read in pre-school and do advanced algebra in kindergarten. Well, maybe it just seems that way. But back in the Stone Age when I was in kindergarten, we learned more of the basics – like how to nap, play nice, and not eat the paste.

I was reminded of those basic relational skills this past Valentine's Day when I read some words offered by Pope Francis. He was speaking to an audience of 25,000 people when he suggested the following recipe for marital success – three simple words – "Please, thanks, and sorry." Now you may be thinking – "Well duh, everybody knows that." Really? We may have all learned it at one time or another but have often forgotten just how much power those words pack.

These basic skills of 1) making a polite request (instead of a demand), 2) expressing gratitude (instead of criticism), and 3) apologizing (instead of blaming), can reinvigorate a marriage. When we are on the receiving end of "please, thanks, and sorry," we love it and wish there was more of it. So why do we have such difficulty offering these words to those we love?

There could be a hundred different reasons that we might give to explain our resistance. Yet acquiring that insight or explaining our behavior doesn't really matter. What matters is using these words to let our spouse know that we respect them enough to be polite, grateful, and appropriately apologetic.

Purposeful Action: Try these words that we learned in kindergarten (and from the pope): if you want something from your spouse, say "Please;" if he or she does something nice for you, say "Thanks;" and if you make a mistake (which we all do), say "I'm sorry." Not revolutionary words, but they could revolutionize your relationship.

 *Day 85*

What are the Rules for Engagement?

Scripture – "Encourage one another, be of one mind, live in peace. And the God of love and peace will be with you." 2 Corinthians 13:11b

We have looked in previous days at how technology impacts our most precious relationships. In recent years, cells phones have begun to occupy greater and greater prominence in our lives. While it certainly puts the world at our fingertips, it also has contributed to incredible strain on our most significant relationships. We have examined the resulting distance, isolation, and loneliness that so often occurs.

While technology has enhanced our lives in so many ways, we certainly do not want it to do so at the expense of our marriages. So today I want to simply offer some healthy ways to approach this conundrum. And I would suggest that discovering functional rules of engagement is not difficult – it is accepting and implementing them that is.

Purposeful Action: Rules of Engagement

- Discuss with your mate your desires and expectations around technology use by you and your partner.

- Discuss your desires with regard to use in the car?

- Discuss what, if any, places in the home are off-limits to electronic devices?

- Discuss the level of privacy or transparency you desire when it comes to texting, email, and Facebook accounts.

- Be intentional about eliminating the "fractured consciousness" mentality in your relationship. In others words, have regular times where technology is not even visible.

- Set aside times of day, as well as days, and perhaps even certain weekends – when technology is absolutely offline.

I know that some of these recommendations may seem extreme in our "virtual world" driven culture. But they are not, if we are committed to making our significant relationship – well – significant. It is important that we learn to "be of one mind" or come to an agreement in this area.

Day 86

Do You Have Earworms?

Scripture – "Gracious words are a honeycomb, sweet to the soul and healing to the bones." Proverbs 16:24

"That's it! I knew it. My kids had ear infections or lice or something last week and I think they somehow gave it to my wife, and now I've got it! I should have known!" No, no, no. This is not some kind of creepy crawling thing in your ear (even though it does sort of sound that way).

Have you ever had those times when you hear a song and can't get the tune out of your head? Perhaps it was "Can't Stop Believin'" by Journey or The Jackson 5's "ABC." It seems like no matter how hard you try, you just can't stop singing in your head "ABC, It's easy as 1,2,3 . . ." Well, these are what psychologists refer to as "earworms."

As researchers have analyzed the kinds of songs that become "earworms" they found that those tunes that were up-beat, had familiar melody, and had a uniqueness about them were more likely to get into the "repeat loop" in our brains.

As I read about this, I couldn't help but wonder if the same isn't true in our marriages. What makes you look forward to coming home to be with your spouse? For me personally, I always know that she is going to be glad to see me (up-tempo), she is a familiar and comfortable place for me (familiar melody), and she is my wife and woman like no other (unique). I find that the more those characteristics are true, the more my spouse is like those stuck tunes in my head (I can't bring myself to call her an "earworm." Any word with "worm" in it just seems like a poor comparison. But you get the point.)

My question for you to ponder though is, are you striving to become a pleasantly stuck tune in your mate's head? Are you an up-beat, familiar, unique welcoming place for him or her?

Purposeful Action: Most all of us want our mates to have pleasant thoughts about us during the day and perhaps even miss us. Ask yourself – "What is one thing I can do today that would cause my spouse to have me stuck in their head (in a positive way), and would in turn create anticipation for our return home this evening." Ponder, contemplate, meditate about it – but more importantly, do what you need to do to become an earworm.

Day 87

Flirting

Scripture – "Above all else, guard your heart, for everything you do flows from it." Proverbs 4:23

She came into my office loaded for bear. The previous weekend she and her husband had gone to his company Christmas party. While there, one of her husband's co-workers began to talk with him. She giggled as they recounted "inside" jokes and stories regarding customers. In the course of the conversation, she even touched his arm a couple of times with a familiarity that drove his wife up the wall.

As you can imagine, his wife did her best to put on an appropriate smile for the party, but inside she was smoldering. As they drove home, icicles hung in the air. Her husband was aware of the tension but was actually a bit clueless as to why she was so withdrawn. Arriving home, he casually asked, "Are you ok?" It was as though he had lit the fuse on a stick of dynamite. She exploded on him about what she observed and how she felt. Whether in the position of the husband or the wife – some of you have been there.

Why does flirting garner this kind of reaction? Because it feels like a violation. While you may not be able to put your finger on it at the time, you clearly feel as though your spouse is giving something to another that should be meant only for you. And you react.

Purposeful Action: Intimate and playful joking should be reserved for your spouse. But here is the cool thing – it can be. Do you want to flirt? Super! You can, and it can be lots of fun – with your mate. I am sure that in the past you flirted with your husband or wife. And the great thing is – you can do it again. Even though you may be out of practice, I want to encourage you to revisit flirting with your spouse. If it has been a while, you may have to practice. But oh what fun that can be! It doesn't have to be anything elaborate, but engage in some type of flirting behavior <u>today</u> with your partner.

 *Day 88*

Admit it and Shut Up

Scripture – "Love does not boast, it is not proud. It is not rude, it is not easily angered, it keeps no record of wrongs." I Corinthians 13:4-5

You just got home from the dentist and told your wife that he wanted $200 to fix a tooth. While he had explained to you the risk of waiting to get it fixed, such as breaking the tooth and then needing a root canal, you just don't want to shell out the money right now. Your wife warns you that waiting is a bad idea. I'll bet you can almost predict what happened next. Yep, three weeks went by and one afternoon he bit into a sandwich and "crack," the tooth was broken in half.

Now, if you are like so many of us, the way that we handle that situation is comical, if we weren't so serious about it. That husband went home in pain and complaining that this wouldn't have happened if the sandwich shop had used fresher bread, and the wife couldn't resist saying, "I told you so." Needless to say, big icicles hung off their words for the rest of the evening.

This scenario has played itself out repeatedly in home after home. So what might be a more productive solution? Ogden Nash said, "To keep your marriage brimming, with love in the wedding cup, whenever you're wrong, admit it; whenever you're right, shut up."

Profound words in a little rhyme.

Purposeful Action: If we will learn those two skills, we will be much further ahead in our marriages: 1) when we make a mistake, rather than deflect blame, people respect us far more when we just admit and own it; and 2) when we have cautioned or given advice that has gone unheeded, but is later proven to be correct, we are far more helpful and loving when we listen with understanding and say nothing. I encourage you to try these strategies today.

 *Day 89*

Actions Trump Words

Scripture – "What good is it, my brothers and sisters, if someone claims to have faith but has no deeds? Can such faith save them? Suppose a brother or a sister is without clothes and daily food. If one of you says to them, 'Go in peace; keep warm and well fed,' but does nothing about their physical needs, what good is it? In the same way, faith by itself, if it is not accompanied by action, is dead." James 2:14-17

I recently sat with a couple who were in the heat of a disagreement. They had an argument that morning that had begun small - over a misunderstood comment but was then followed with the phrase "You don't support me." From there things went downhill at full throttle. But why? He was completely offended and felt invalidated by this comment. In trying to discuss what happened, he found it very difficult to get his head around the issue. He kept saying, "I do support her, I do love her, she is a priority." Yet, those words seemed to fall on deaf ears.

It wasn't that she didn't hear the words, because she did. It was that she had heard them before – over and over. But the words were not backed up with concrete and congruent actions. Instead, he would say these words but then continue in his self-centered behaviors that were not supportive of her, that did not make her a priority. Yet, he then seemed bewildered that she did not believe his words. Why? Because he missed out on an important concept – **actions always trump words!**

Don't misunderstand me and think that affirming words are not important, because they are. But in order to be believable and valued and accepted by the person hearing them, they must be backed up by consistent actions. Think about it – when you are sent two different and conflicting messages – one by words and one by behavior or actions – which one do you believe? No doubt, it is what you clearly see over what you might hear. It was true when we were kids (and is true for our kids) and is no less true for us as adults. Your loved one likes to hear words of support when they know that they can count on you to back up those words with tangible supportive behavior.

Purposeful Action: What can you do today to begin to be believable? Recall something you may have said to your spouse recently that perhaps elicited an eye roll. No doubt, that was a result of their having heard the words before but did not see follow through with actions. Intentionally engage in behavior today that clearly backs up previously spoken words. This is the first step to creating a foundation of trustworthiness.

Day 90

Why Bother?

Scripture – "Greater love has no one than this: to lay down one's life for one's friends." John 15:13

Oh the things that we stumble onto when we are cleaning out. A couple of weeks ago I was going through some old books when I came across a grocery store coupon that was inside one of them. All I can figure is that at some point in time, when I was reading it, I must have needed a book mark and grabbed this coupon to use.

The coupon is for Imperial margarine and is redeemable for 7 cents. No that is not a mistake – 7 cents. Of course I should add that the expiration date on the coupon is December 31, 1973. When sharing this story with my oldest son, he responded with "7 cents – why bother?" And that is an easy question to understand – in 2017. But in 1973, 7 cents was worth something and actually made a difference in your grocery shopping budget. The coupon had value that today we would dismiss as pretty worthless.

I wonder how many of us have taken a view of our

spouse as though he or she were an old 7 cent coupon? They had great value to us when we married them in 1973 - or 1950, 2005, or whatever year you walked down the aisle. But in today's relational economy we may not view, talk to, or treat our spouse as though they have the same value that they did when we first encountered them. And if we don't treat him or her like they have value, for all intents and purposes, for us, they don't have.

Jesus states, "Where your treasure is there your heart will be also," Matthew 6:21. Unlike the 7 cent coupon, the value of our spouse did not expire in 1973, even though we may act as though it did. My hope today that you will reconsider the great value of your husband or wife.

Purposeful Action: Staying with the theme of coupons, I want to suggest that you create some type of coupon book for your spouse. These could be simply hand-drawn or, if you are more creative with the computer, you could design and print them out. But whichever you do, create at least five redeemable coupons. Some examples might be: "This coupon is good for one foot massage;" or "This coupon can be redeemed for a picnic at the park of your choice;" or "Good for one breakfast in bed." Get creative. What is important isn't so much the individual items on the coupons as much as the fact that the book communicates that your spouse is worth the effort. That is why we bother.

Day 91

An Opportunity

Scripture – "And we know that in all things God works for the good of those who love him, who have been called according to his purpose." Romans 8:28

In recent months I have had the chance to see the movie "Lincoln." Aside from tremendous acting on the part of the star-studded cast, I was moved by the character of a man such as Lincoln. It is easy to make a statement such as that based upon the resistance he encountered as he worked to free the slaves. But I want to look this morning at the relationship in the back story.

If you have seen the move, you may recall some tense exchanges between President Lincoln and his wife Mary. Mary was known for many things: intense impulses, an unbridled temper, and sometimes out of control spending sprees. And yet, even with these difficulties, Lincoln was a principled man who held together a nation that was coming apart at the seams.

I have heard many man and woman talk about difficult and challenging qualities they find in their spouses. You may fit into that category – living with a spouse who is a control freak, an alcoholic, or is constantly demeaning. You may feel that God could do great things in your life and through you if you just weren't limited by this unbearable and impossible spouse. Yet, the reality is that

God may be using your spouse (as hard as this may be to accept) to mold and shape you spiritually in a manner that prepares you for exactly what He wants you to do. You may be about to experience a season of incredible spiritual growth.

Lincoln's marriage did not prevent him from achieving greatness. As a matter of fact, the difficulties in his marriage, and the demonstration of his character to not give up, may have been the exact quality that was needed to keep this fragile nation together and set it on a course of restoration.

Purposeful Action: As you ponder the relationship with your spouse, what are you learning and how is this causing you to grow? Identify one struggle with your spouse that is particularly difficult. It is easy to point out the unfairness of it all and complain that your spouse is somehow holding you back. But pray about and ask God to show you how He wants to use this issue to stretch you. If you will listen closely, you just may find that God is growing you for great things.

Index of Topics

Index of Scripture

Matthew 6:14 – Day 70
Matthew 6:21 – Day 22
Matthew 7:4-5 – Day 30
Matthew 7:24-27 - Day 46
Mark 10:8 – Day 23
Mark 10:15-16 – Day 28
Luke 6:31 – Day 72
Luke 6:45 – Day 35
Luke 10:41-42 – Day 11
John 13:12-14 – Day 82
John 13:34 – Day 73
John 13:35 – Day 84
John 15:12 – Day 1
John 15:13 – Day 90
Romans 5:3-4 – Day 32
Romans 8:28 – Day 91
Romans 12:2 – Day 13
Romans 12:10 – Day 10
Romans 12:15 – Day 49
Romans 14:19 – Day 53
Romans 15:1-2 – Day 14
Romans 15:7 – Day 9
I Corinthians 1:10 – Day 36
I Corinthians 13: 4 & 5 – Day 88
I Corinthians 13:7-8a – Day 4
I Corinthians 13:11-12a – Day 63
I Corinthians 16:14 – Day 20
2 Corinthians 5:17 – Day 21
2 Corinthians 10:5 – Day 67
2 Corinthians 13:11b - Day 85
Galatians 5:22-23 – Day 41
Ephesians 1:16 – Day 31
Ephesians 4:2 – Day 78
Ephesians 4:16 – Day 29

ABOUT THE AUTHOR

BARRY D. HAM, Ph.D. is a college professor, marriage and family therapist and an author and speaker. He received an MS in Psychology from Abilene Christian University, followed by a Masters in Marriage and Family Counseling from California State University. He received his PH.D. in Clinical Psychology from Southern California University. He lives in the Colorado Springs area with his wife and their two Goldendoodles. He and his wife have grown children whose families live in Colorado and Florida, and they have three grandkids.

CONTACT INFORMATION

Dr. Ham is available to speak at your church or gathering and also available for weekend seminars.

For booking and additional information, he can be contacted at:

Dr. Barry D. Ham

c/o Integrative Family/Individual Therapy

P.O. Box 63241

Colorado Springs, CO 80962

drbdham@msn.com

www.livingonpurpose.net

Made in United States
North Haven, CT
28 September 2023

42097882R00125